Eleftherios Venizelos

Eleftherios Venizelos
Greece
Andrew Dalby

First published in Great Britain in 2010 by
Haus Publishing Ltd
70 Cadogan Place
London SW1X 9AH
www.hauspublishing.com

Copyright © Andrew Dalby, 2010

The moral right of the author has been asserted

A CIP catalogue record for this book
is available from the British Library

ISBN 978-1-905791-64-4

Series design by Susan Buchanan
Typeset in Sabon by MacGuru Ltd
Printed in Dubai by Oriental Press
Map by Martin Lubikowski, ML Design, London

Contents

Acknowledgements   vi
Note on dates etc.   vii
Prologue   ix

I The Life and the Land   1
1 A Revolutionary by Profession   3
2 Princely Crete   18
3 Liberal Greece   33
4 The National Schism   55

II The Paris Peace Conference   77
5 Preparing for Paris   79
6 At the Conference   98
7 The Catastrophe and the Treaty of Lausanne   122

III The Legacy   143
8 Venizelos's Later Career   145

Notes   160
Chronology   180
Further Reading   198
Picture Sources   207
Index   209

Acknowledgements

In working on this brief life of Venizelos I have been grateful for suggestions by Jaqueline Mitchell and Alan Sharp, which have improved it in many ways, and for discussions with Dimitri Michalopoulos, of the Eleftherios Venizelos Historical Foundation in Athens. A grant from the Society of Authors was, in a different way, just as helpful.

Note on dates etc.

Translations from books in Greek and French are mine unless stated otherwise; the notes also cite existing translations where this may be useful.

In this book, because of its international context, dates are always given according to the Gregorian (new style) calendar. As a result, dates here will differ (by 12 days before 1900, and by 13 days thereafter) from those in certain other sources which follow the Julian (old style) calendar used in Greece until 1 March 1923. When citing specific documents originating in Greece and therefore dated in the old style, I provide both dates. Thus, in the case of the 'Letter of 13/25 March 1878' cited in Chapter 1, Note 5 the document carries the date 13 March 1878, which was 25 March new style.

I use the term 'prime minister' even for times and places where the current title was an equivalent of 'president of the council'. I use the term 'ambassador' even where the current title was 'minister' or 'minister plenipotentiary'.

Eleftherios Venizelos (1864–1936) on his arrival in Salonica in Ocotber 1916 as head of the pro-Allied provisional government.

Prologue

A lawyer's voice, soft, precise, controlled, without excessive emotion. He spoke the Greek of one who had learned to love the ancient authors, Greek that was classical in grammar and sometimes a little pedantic in choice of words. Greek apart, he could manage German and English but he preferred French. His French accent, claimed by admirers to be fault-less, was said by critical observers to be far from perfect; but all statesmen used French, and many spoke it much worse than Venizelos did.

It cannot have been the voice alone. It was also the eyes, no doubt. Bright, darting eyes, that peered through gold-rimmed spectacles with the expression of a scholar – of one accustomed to studying ancient manuscripts – rather than a political pugilist; yet they looked you straight in the eye and somehow seemed to read your innermost thoughts. And the hair, prematurely white and thin; the trim white beard; the lips, full, mobile, sensitive; the gentle smile, expressive of patience and sympathy, and once described as 'bitter-sweet'. When he smiled his whole face seemed to light up with benev-olence and friendship.

And then there was what he had to say; always reasonable

and even-handed, surprisingly moderate, seemingly unarguable; nearly always ideally phrased – though without apparent calculation – to win over any listener who happened not to share his views.

The charisma and fearsome persuasiveness of Eleftherios Venizelos derived not from any one of these qualities but from all of them together. He knew his own skills and was wise enough to see that if he overused them his audience might incline against him in an attempt to be fair. He was at his best and most persuasive when – as on this particular evening, 28 January 1919 – he was speaking not one-to-one but as the host of a small group, some of whom were already acolytes. Venizelos liked to play host.

Commander Gerald Talbot was one of the group. A convinced Venizelist from some years back,[1] he had been dispatched from London to the British Legation in Athens, as Naval Attaché, just two weeks earlier. His first duty had been to trundle back to Paris in Venizelos's train to act as liaison between the Greeks and the British at the Paris Peace Conference. Also present was Harold Nicolson, a technical adviser on the British delegation. He had met Venizelos for the first time a few days earlier, and it is his diary that records this private dinner. He would soon be writing, in a letter to his father, that Venizelos and Lenin were 'the only two really great men in Europe.'[2]

> 'I can't tell you the position that Venizelos has here! He and Lenin are the only two really great men in Europe.'
>
> HAROLD NICOLSON AT THE PARIS PEACE CONFERENCE

There was plenty of space at the Hôtel Mercédès, where the Greek delegation, around 25 strong, had taken three floors, enough to accommodate 80 guests;[3] but Venizelos's sitting-room was modest enough, very cosy – a little stuffy, in fact. It looked north along the avenue Kléber and into the place de l'Etoile. The vast circle was busy even by night, bright on this winter evening with street lamps and carriage lanterns; the Arc de Triomphe shone at its centre.

His listeners were not distracted by any of this. Venizelos was 'in great form'. They listened spellbound as he recounted his developing quarrel with King Constantine, which broke out in 1914 and climaxed in Constantine's ignominious exile three years later. Told in Venizelos's words this story seemed almost more real and crucial than the First World War, its backdrop. Stories of the King's 'lies and equivocations' led on to a retelling of certain earlier episodes with Constantine's brother, Prince George, the former High Commissioner of Crete who had driven Venizelos, his Councillor for Justice, to armed rebellion in 1905. *I escaped to the mountains*, Venizelos recalled, and added that this was when he had taught himself English, reading *The Times* with a rifle across his knees; admittedly he once claimed, to a different audience, that this was when he had perfected his French.[4] From that topic he turned to another just as close to his heart: the modern Greek language and its relation to the speech of ancient Athens. His guests persuaded him, not unwillingly, to recite passages from the ancient Homeric epics. 'An odd effect,' Nicolson thought, 'rather moving'.[5]

It had been a long journey to the warm hotels and draughty conference rooms of Paris. The radical lawyer and journalist born in Crete in 1864 had finally steered his native island to union with Greece; he himself had made the astonishing leap to Greek party leader and Prime Minister. And at last, against all the odds, he had led Greece into the First World War on the winning side. In 1919, a respected international figure, a name and face recognised by newspaper readers worldwide, Eleftherios Venizelos was among those who would decide the fate of the defeated belligerents and the future shape of Europe. Cursed by many at home for having split the nation and driven the King into exile, he needed to redeem himself by bringing home the prizes that Greece had fought for.

YUGOSLAVIA

Belgrade

ROMANIA

Bucharest

DOBRUDJA

BULGARIA

Sofia

Edirne
(Adrianople)

WESTERN
THRACE

To GREECE 1920-23
INTERNATIONAL
ZONE

ALBANIA

NORTHERN
EPIRUS

M A C E D O N I A   Kavala

EASTERN
THRACE

Alexandroupolis

Istanbul
(Constantinople)

Korçë

Gjirokastër

Salonica

Ioannina

EPIRUS

Corfu

THESSALY

Lemnos

Mudanya

Bursa

Aegean Sea

Lesbos

Chios

To GREECE
after transition

Afyonkarahisar

Athens

Izmir (Smyrna)

IONIA

Samos

Aydın

Syros

ITALIAN Z

Antalya

Cythera

DODECANESE

Rhodes

Chania

Iraklio

Crete

M e d i t e r r a n e a n   S e a

Turkey, Greece and Bulgaria 1912–1923

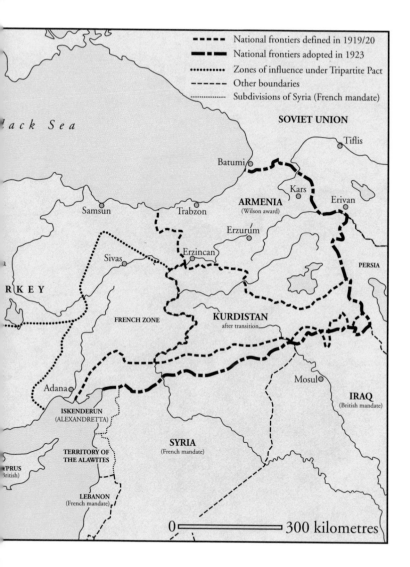

National frontiers defined in 1919/20
National frontiers adopted in 1923
Zones of influence under Tripartite Pact
Other boundaries
Subdivisions of Syria (French mandate)

Black Sea

SOVIET UNION

Tiflis

Batumi

Kars

Samsun

Trabzon

ARMENIA
(Wilson award)

Erivan

Erzurum

Erzincan

PERSIA

Sivas

TURKEY

FRENCH ZONE

KURDISTAN
after transition

Adana

Mosul

IRAQ
(British mandate)

ISKENDERUN
(ALEXANDRETTA)

SYRIA
(French mandate)

TERRITORY OF
THE ALAWITES

CYPRUS
(British)

LEBANON
(French mandate)

0 _____ 300 kilometres

Eleftherios Venizelos *circa* 1900.

I

The Life and the Land

1

A Revolutionary by Profession

The Greek mainland and the great island of Crete were politically separated, yet they shared a majority language and culture. Greek speakers in Greece and Crete called themselves *Roméi*; the Eastern Roman Empire that this name recalls – the Byzantine Empire, as we call it – had been destroyed by the Ottoman Turks when they captured the Greek metropolis of Constantinople in 1453. Greeks and Cretans fought together in the successful uprising against Turkish rule that broke out in 1821 and resulted, after nine years, in the creation of a small independent state of Greece. But Constantinople was still the capital of the Ottoman Empire, and Crete remained an Imperial possession. Throughout the 19th century, down to 1905, the island's history was studded with a series of armed uprisings. Each rebellion brought more social and economic turmoil. Cumulatively they led to a reluctant Ottoman recognition of special status for Crete – Christian, Greek-speaking, increasingly autonomous.

Resistance to change was built into the Ottoman state, but in Crete there was a good reason for it. With each rebellion and each political concession, the originally prosperous Muslim population of the island, 25 per cent of 280,000 in 1880 and contributing far more than 25 per cent of the tax revenues of the province, became more nervous about its future. Muslim emigration gathered pace. Thirty years later the population reached 300,000; Muslims now formed scarcely 10 per cent of it. Trade faltered; tax revenue fell.

A letter apparently written by Eleftherios Venizelos himself told of the part played by his father, Kyriakos, in these struggles. *When still very young he took part in the great uprising of 1821: he was secretary to Koumis, the chieftain from Selinos, at the siege of Monemvasia. He was awarded the bronze medal of the uprising. Three of his brothers fell in that holy war; another, Chatzi-Nikolos Benizelos, was one of three Cretans who were sent to negotiate with the Greek leaders when the rebellion first broke out ... Exiled in 1843 by the Turkish government, which confiscated his property and business assets, he remained an outlaw for a full 19 years.*[1] In 1821 Kyriakos Venizelos would have been a mere boy, useful to the revolutionaries as a messenger or because he could write. Monemvasia fell – one of the first great successes of the uprising – in July of that year.

The Ottoman Empire was ruled from Constantinople (İstanbul) by its hereditary Sultans, descendants of Mehmed II, the victor of 1453. It was an Islamic empire, though religious minorities were tolerated; its peoples spoke many languages, but Turkish was paramount. During the 19th century the Empire's European territories steadily shrank as one national state after another gained independence – Greece among them.

Crete, Venizelos's native island, was the Ottoman province of *Girit*. Its capital, Chania, may well be the most ancient continuously-inhabited city in Europe. The central district of Chania was completely enclosed by massive Venetian-built walls; its gates were closed at nightfall.

The real antecedents and history of Kyriakos Venizelos are far from clear. He was a Greek citizen, not a Cretan, on close terms with successive Greek consuls at Chania;[2] but in 1846 he married Styliani Ploumidaki from the mountain village of Theriso and started a family. Styliani never learned to read or write. They had nine children of whom six survived infancy, four girls and two boys. Their first son, Agathoklis, was handicapped. Eleftherios, the younger son, was born in 1864, and by that time Kyriakos was a prominent tradesman with a general store in the Topanas quarter of Chania. He was also president of the Minos Club and trustee of the Greek School. The family lived over the shop in the winter and had another house where they spent the summer at Mournies, five kilometres to the south, one of the ten orange-growing villages that encircle Chania; behind them the land rises sharply towards the rugged White Mountains.

Eleftherios was born at Mournies on the night of 23/24 August. His parents, overjoyed to have a healthy baby boy but fearful of evil, took a special precaution. Immediately after his birth he was wrapped and placed outside the house door. In the early morning of 24 August Kyriakos brought the 'foundling' indoors and persuaded Styliani that they should 'adopt' him. It was on 24 August that Eleftherios Venizelos always celebrated his birthday.[3] Early biographers claimed that the name Eleftherios, chosen by the village priest, means 'liberator' and was a political choice (its actual meaning, 'free-spirited' or 'liberal', coincides neatly with the political party he was to found) but in truth he was named after the village's patron saint.

Just two years later another rebellion broke out. Kyriakos opposed it, and in August 1866 fled from Crete with his family. The details of their journey are not known. For many Cretans it was a two- or three-day trek across the bleak and massive mountain spine of Crete to one of the southern beaches, and then a hungry and uncomfortable vigil, sheltering in caves or under cliffs. Almost every night, somewhere along the coast (but no one knew in advance where it would be), a Greek ship would land volunteers, arms and other supplies paid for by well-wishers and would pick up refugees for its return journey. They had a hard time of it. A foreign eye-witness estimated that by the end of this rebellion there were 60,000 Cretans in Greece, most of them living in poverty, many girls and young women surviving by prostitution.[4] The Venizelos family disembarked at the first landfall, the island of Cythera, and were not among the most unlucky. It was here that Eleftherios would get to know Kostis Foumis, afterwards his co-conspirator in the 1905 rebellion, and Klearchos Markantonakis who was to be his confidential friend and private secretary. In 1866 Cythera was a crossroads of Greek maritime transport, a stopping point for vessels plying between Greece and Crete and a port of call for ships from Italy on their way east. Culturally and politically the island was a curiosity: until just two years previously it had formed part of the United States of the Ionian Islands, a now-forgotten European outpost of the British Empire.

After three years in Cythera the family shifted to another island crossroads, Syros, the busiest port of the middle Aegean. In this cosmopolitan little city, rising like an amphitheatre around its bustling harbour, they stayed for another three years. Syros was where Eleftherios first went to school, and where his youngest sister, Evanthia, was born.

In summer 1872 Kyriakos Venizelos brought his family back to Chania. He now ran a general store with a special line in glassware, in narrow, busy Chalidon Street opposite the Capuchin convent (where women travellers stayed, since Chania had no hotels). Eleftherios is said to have been a leader among boys of his age and a poetry-lover. 'Crete doesn't need any more songs or guns,' Kyriakos commented severely. 'It has plenty of both.' Wishing his son to be trained in business, he took on the heavy financial burden of sending the boy, aged 13, as a boarder to a private commercial school in Athens.

Eleftherios spent two years there, 1877 to 1879, and wrote home often. One letter, touching on Athenian politics, criticised Alexandros Koumoundouros (Prime Minister for most of that period) and praised his opponent, the moderate Charilaos Trikoupis. 'Just worry about your studies and your health,' his father replied. 'Pay no attention to newspaper gossip.'[5] For his last school year Eleftherios was moved again, back to Syros where the public *gymnasion* (grammar school) was one of the best in Greece and was free to the sons of Greek citizens. His father was now building a new family house and was hardly able to afford a third year of private education; a long, frank letter by Eleftherios, complaining of his *unbearable life* at the commercial school, was probably the deciding factor.[6]

In late 1880 the building work was finished and the family moved out from the crowded old streets of Chania to a spacious new house on the rural edge of the city, prominently sited among the foreign consulates and just above the little fishing harbour of Chalepa. In the same year Eleftherios's elder sister married. It was a good marriage. Konstantinos Mitsotakis, 15 years older than Ekaterina, was leader of the *Xipoliti* (the 'Barefeet' or liberals) in the provincial Cretan Assembly and editor of the Chania weekly paper *Lefka Ori*, 'White Mountains'.

It is said that Eleftherios wanted to go on to university, that Kyriakos opposed it, and that his friend and neighbour, the

Greek consul, persuaded him that times had changed; where he had prospered through trade his son would thrive on an Athens law degree. The comparison between a shopkeeper's income and a lawyer's may have entered into the calculation. At any rate, in October 1880 Eleftherios returned to Athens to register as an undergraduate.[7]

He alternated study in Athens and work in the family shop and began his second year only in 1882; but he worked hard, eventually giving up his place in the noisy house that seven Cretan students shared and taking a room near the law school. He found time none the less to reflect on Koumoundouros's funeral in March 1883, and on opposition complaints that the Premier had unduly favoured his political friends. *Yes, maybe he feigned ignorance of minor instances of corruption ... it's not Koumoundouros but the system that is to blame, a system that impels deputies to influence administrative decisions.*[8] These were the hidden imperatives of political patronage: Greek party politics were built on personal followings, not on principles. In June Eleftherios was called home to attend his father's deathbed. He now became head of the family, with his mother, his unmarried sister Evanthia and his handicapped brother Agathoklis all dependent on him; and they were nearly bankrupt. His father had overreached himself. Eleftherios had no choice but to stay at home and run the shop. Thanks to the regular steamers between Chania and Piraeus he managed to attend a minimum number of classes in Athens. In 1885 he felt able to sell up and undertake two final years of full-time study, a risk that would pay off if he could get his doctorate and make a career in law. That is surely what his father would have told him to do.

As early as 1884 he was active in student politics. Two years later came an encounter with a British politician, the dissident

Liberal Joseph Chamberlain, who was visiting Greece on his way home from a fact-finding visit to Constantinople and had been interviewed for the Athens daily *Akropolis*. As regards Crete, Chamberlain said, he was assured by a Greek highly placed in the Ottoman government that the Greeks of the island wanted independence, not union with Greece.

In reality Greece and Crete had shared too many of the trials and tragedies of rebellion; neither would ever be satisfied with an autonomous Crete, still less an independent Crete. To Greeks these concepts were anathema: a Greater Greece, desired and demanded by almost all who took any interest in politics, must surely include Crete. Among Cretans, it was true, some spoke for *Enosis* ('Union') and some argued merely for autonomy, but even these latter never failed to hint (when addressing Cretan audiences) that autonomy would be the prelude to union. The difference was not in the aim but in the approach, bearing in mind that an Ottoman subject who proposed local autonomy was a nuisance, while one who urged union with a hostile neighbouring country was a traitor. Whether or not Chamberlain realised in advance how hot the issue was, his unnamed informant in Constantinople certainly did.

Akropolis printed the interview on 1/13 November 1886. Cretan students in Athens were outraged, and sent a five-man deputation to Chamberlain to tell him the true state of opinion. The result was a long and serious question-and-answer session at the Hôtel d'Angleterre on Syntagma Square; if the students were awed by their reception in one of the best suites in one of the best hotels in Athens, no sign of this appears in the full report that they submitted to the *Nea Efimeris* or 'New Daily'. There was talk of the Cretan Assembly's impotence, of taxes that ought to be spent locally but went to Constantinople, of a so-called free press whose journalists risked imprisonment and death. But was it true, Chamberlain asked them, that the Cretan Assembly had voted for union with Greece? If so, why was this not reported in Europe? If it was true that journalists were treated harshly, he demanded, why had members of the Assembly escaped punishment for this seditious vote? As his student interlocutors answered these questions the dialogue appears to have shifted perspective, confidently dissecting the inertia politics of Britain, France, Italy and Russia (the 'Powers') that sustained the Ottoman government (the 'Porte').

> 'If there is no rebellion in Crete today, it is because Cretans know that Europe would act against them ... This does not prevent our being in a state of 'chronic revolution'.'
>
> **VENIZELOS TO JOSEPH CHAMBERLAIN**

Your information is correct. This year, just five months ago, the Assembly voted unanimously for Union. For some time now the consuls of the Powers in Chania have refused to accept submissions from any Cretan representative bodies; yet the vote was reported in the local press. But the Porte will not risk the provocation of using force against all the people's representatives at once. Turkish power, sir, is exercised in Crete with the moral support of Europe ... If there is no rebellion in Crete today, it is because Cretans know that Europe would act against them, just as it did against Greece this year. This does not prevent our being in a state of chronic revolution, as one of your colleagues in the House of Commons aptly put it.

'Chronic revolution' turns out to be a quotation, and an astonishingly apposite one. These words were spoken five months earlier in the widely-reported Irish Home Rule debate in the House of Commons on 7 June 1886, in a brief intervention by a Conservative, alluding to Crete as an island currently 'in the news'. Gladstone, then Liberal Prime Minister, angrily challenged the words: '"Give me a test of chronic revolution. Has Crete paid its tribute? Has it called for the armed forces of Turkey to put down revolution?" (Cries of "Yes".)' [9] Chamberlain himself had just resigned from his ministerial post on the Irish issue and was in the thick of the parliamentary battle; by voting with the Conservatives at the end of this debate he brought down the Liberal government.

Nothing justifies the claim by Doros Alastos, his English biographer, that 'Venizelos led the delegation'; nothing justifies reprinting the interview with all of the delegation's questions and answers attributed to Venizelos, as Ioannis Manolikakis and others have done. [10] All we can say for sure is that Venizelos was one of the five students. But the clever use of words specially relevant to an interlocutor, stored in memory from avid reading of the newspapers, is so typical of his later style of argument that this particular response can surely be attributed to him. Here he is already at his best. At his worst, he would press a point until he had made an enemy. At his *viva* in January 1887 he fielded a criticism in Roman Law from Professor Krassas, was defended by Professor Kostis, and refused to give way on the grounds that he could never satisfy both. Unfortunately Roman Law was Krassas's subject. Venizelos's cheekiness was the reason – so he later claimed – why his doctorate was graded 'very good' instead of 'best'.

Did he fall ill with typhoid fever immediately after this incident? Convalescence would help to explain his aimlessness on returning to Chania: playing whist with Alfred Biliotti, the British Consul in Chalepa; riding on donkey-back to Chania and strolling fashionably beside the harbour; failing to be elected as local appeal judge; studying German with the vague aim of continuing his studies abroad; and, eventually, falling in love with Maria Katelouzou, daughter of a prosperous olive oil merchant whose family also had a foothold at Smyrna, the great Greek metropolis of Asia Minor.

Love, perhaps, renewed his energy. He played the guitar and Maria sang; he forgot the fantasy of foreign study and joined the law firm of Spyros Moatsos in Chania. Law was to provide his income through nearly all of the years 1887 to 1909. Whenever politics left him no time for law, the money ran out.

At the end of 1888, when his brother-in-law gave up editing the weekly *Lefka Ori*, Venizelos took over in collaboration with his friend Kostis Foumis and two colleagues. On most Mondays for the next seven months a leading article by Venizelos appeared, transparently signed *Lefkoritis*, 'White Mountaineer'. In March 1889 he and his co-editors campaigned in the elections for the Cretan Assembly. On 15 April (exactly three months after his engagement to Maria) all four were elected, in Crete's first ever secret ballot. They ranged themselves with Mitsotakis's liberals but were soon seen as breasting a new wave in Cretan politics. Ioannis Gryparis, the new Greek Consul, reported to Athens on 'members from the districts of Chania and Sfakia, young professionals from the *Lefka Ori* group. Although they belong to the liberal majority they openly distance themselves … from the deplorable behaviour of their colleagues from the eastern constituencies. These few young men, eight or ten in all, have regrettably not been able to carry their views on every issue, but they have often succeeded in moderating the wilder excesses of the majority.'[11] It did not last. Two days after this report, the *Karnavades* ('Carpetbaggers' or conservatives), now commanding fewer than one-fourth of the seats, seized the initiative by forcing an Assembly vote on immediate union with Greece. The liberals were wrong-footed by this opportunism. Few could bring themselves to oppose the union that they had regularly demanded while in opposition. Venizelos and his group, heeding the Greek government's advice transmitted by Gryparis, alone voted against.

The motion passed overwhelmingly and resulted in immediate widespread violence between Christians and the Muslim minority. Constantinople abruptly recalled the provincial governor, replacing him with a military commander, Shakir Pasha, who declared martial law, arrested political leaders, dissolved the Assembly and restored some Muslim privileges, eventually regaining control. Venizelos and Foumis were not there to see it; they evaded arrest by fleeing from Chania on a moonless night in Biliotti's rowing boat, to be picked up by the Athens steamer hovering offshore. At Athens on the very evening of their arrival they were invited to the Ministry of Finance to meet Prime Minister Trikoupis. Briefed on Gryparis's consular reports he congratulated them as the only Cretan politicians not responsible for the unrest that threatened to nullify his diplomacy.[12]

The most impressive result of Venizelos's brief exile in Athens was his narrative *The Cretan Rebellion of 1889*, which remained in manuscript until 1971.[13] Maria's letters kept him in contact with Chania and the consulates.

Soon after his return to Crete they married, and shared the big house at Chalepa with his mother, and were happy, it is said. Their first son, born in 1893, was named Kyriakos after his paternal grandfather. Eighteen months later a second son was born. Named Sofoklis after his maternal grandfather, the boy was destined, like his father, to serve Greece as Prime

Minister; but Maria died, probably of puerperal fever, nine days after giving birth. She was 24. Inconsolable at her death, Venizelos ever afterwards wore a beard as a sign of mourning.

He continued to practise as a lawyer. In May 1893 he had taken his most notorious case, prosecuting two young Greeks who were accused of murdering the Muslim Tevfik Bedri Bey. They were convicted, publicly hanged at Chania on 19 January 1894, posthumously reprieved, and almost certainly innocent. He stayed away from politics, however. He and his friends had at first not been included in the general amnesty of early 1890, in spite of appeals by Biliotti and others. They had become too prominent. Their sensible journalism and principled stand in the Assembly were far outweighed, in Ottoman eyes, by their unwelcome popularity among the foreign consuls, their notorious escape from arrest and their warm reception by a hostile government. Venizelos kept his head down for five years; at last in early 1895 he and Kostis Foumis began another weekly paper, *Avgi* ('Dawn').

Cretan politics had not stood still; that summer Manousos Koundouros, a young assemblyman who stood apart from the *Lefka Ori* group, gathered a Constitutional Committee which drafted a plan for Crete's future as an autonomous state under a Christian governor with a European police force. The Cretan Assembly withdrew to the hills south of Chania – as it had done several times before – where its acceptance of the Koundouros memorandum marked the outbreak of a new rebellion, with fighting between Muslims and Christians in Chania and skirmishes in the hills. Warships of the four Powers hovered, and by July 1896 the Ottoman government had conceded most of the rebels' demands, but peace did not return. Venizelos sent his mother, his brother Agathoklis and the boys, along with his sister Eleni and her husband, to safety on the Greek island of Milos. He stayed on alone, and in August 1896 risked attending the rebel Assembly at Kambi; there he spoke against rebellion, was attacked for taking cases on behalf of Muslims, and was lucky to escape alive.

In January 1897 a crisis came with violent attacks, apparently government-inspired, on Christian districts of Chania and other towns. Reports of massacres led the Conservative government in Athens, under irresistible public pressure stirred by its own anti-Turkish propaganda, to send troops to Crete to protect the Greeks of the island. This was disastrous for Greece, which thus talked itself into war with the Ottoman Empire, a war it could not win. In Crete, by contrast, the Greek move had two consequences. The 'Powers', British, French, Italian and Russian, fighting to prevent change, prepared to send in troops to restore peace under the tattered Ottoman flag. Meanwhile the Greek Consul, Nikolaos Gennadis, happened to remark to his neighbour Venizelos that (for the first time in 70 years) Greece would actually welcome a Cretan declaration of union.[14] With one eye on the smoke rising from Chania, Venizelos set out with a warlike group from the nearby hill village of Malaxas to join the Assembly's Administrative Committee, which was now encamped not far away at Akrotiri ('the Promontory'). From there, a few days later, he took an armed band westwards to Profitis Ilias Hill, just above Chalepa, and raised the flag of Greece within sight of the European vessels in Chania bay.

Thanks to his contacts with the consuls Venizelos now rapidly gained prominence in a series of complex negotiations during which the admirals of the four Powers found themselves treating the Committee and the rebel Assembly, rather than the Ottoman authorities, as Crete's representatives. When a Russian warship fired on the Greek flag he was among those who signed the protests. 'The banner to which we had rallied, for which every one of us was ready to die, was destroyed by a Christian shell ... We shall pursue the fulfilment of our aims to the death. Long live our King, George I! Long live the Union of Crete with Greece!'[15] He was among those who insisted that no compromise was possible: 'We think it necessary to declare that the only possible, the only just and definitive solution of the Cretan question is the recognition of the Union of Crete with Greece. Any other solution would be nothing but a stopgap.'[16] The Venizelos legend falsely claims that he was there at the hilltop holding aloft the flag under Russian fire, and records a prescient conversation with a British naval officer, who argued: '"If you work with the Powers, your day will come more quickly than by forcing our hand and compelling us to oppose you." *European policy* [Venizelos is said to have replied] *is invariably the maintenance of the status quo, and you will do nothing for the subject races unless we, by taking the initiative, make you realise that helping us against the Turks is the lesser of two evils.* "Damn it all, the beggar is right," wrote the British officer, "and I hope we shan't have to shoot him."'[17]

By June the Powers had had enough of this many-sided conflict and were ready to offer full autonomy for Crete; Greece having ignominiously lost its war, the Cretan rebel Assembly needed to concentrate its demands on reform and autonomy. It was not easy for Venizelos, a fresh convert to union, suddenly to change direction. At a crucial Assembly on 17 August at Archanes, as chairman he attempted to adjourn discussion of the union issue. There was prolonged and violent protest. He was voted out of the chair and refused to take further part. In the night there was an attempt to set fire to the house in which he was staying, and early biographers reported that during his return to Chania he and his party were stoned in many of the villages through which they passed.[18] He retreated, bruised, to Athens. There Prime Minister Trikoupis urged him to finesse his approach to the union issue and put him in touch with the veteran Cretan politician Ioannis Sfakianakis. The two returned to Crete together, and at Melidoni, at an Assembly whose authority was fully recognised by the Admirals of the Powers, Sfakianakis was elected chairman and Venizelos was acclaimed.

His speech, frequently interrupted by applause, is typical of his smooth, classical, occasionally pedantic style: *If our long period of enslavement, and particularly the political vicissitudes of the last ten years … have created disputes among us and sharpened our differences, today we must consign those differences and disputes to perdition; we must now offer our hands to one another, attempting … to awaken to freedom our homeland that has languished in slavery for centuries. What we are to have today does not indeed satisfy the desires of our ancestors, nor the dreams that we ourselves dreamed in our cradles.* He led the Assembly towards acceptance of autonomy, and then, at last, offered the hint expected of every 19th-century Cretan politician … *and thus we shall have taken a very worthwhile step in the fulfilment of our national ideal.* There would be something else, another step beyond.[19]

2
Princely Crete

The coherent principle underlying Venizelos's manoeuvres during his political career in Crete is not obvious. His admirers claim that he unswervingly favoured union; his detractors insist that he backed autonomy, even independence. The disagreement is easy enough to explain. All Greeks in Crete had to speak in favour of union with Greece, whatever their views of its practicality. Venizelos usually did so too; there were, however, sudden and surprising shifts in his position. Therefore it has been claimed that he was a political opportunist. It would be truer to say that he had a 'panel of advisers'; he is usually found to have acted in consort with the Greek Consul and the consuls of the four Powers. Hence his unpopular vote in May 1889 and subsequent exile; hence his sudden decision to give up both law and journalism and become *a revolutionary by profession* in January 1897.[1]

He was walking a tightrope and he knew it. Consuls represent governments. Governments change, and in Greece they change frequently. Union with Crete was on every Greek government's wish list, but it could never be pressed and sometimes it had to be put aside entirely. Greek intervention in

Crete, even the semblance of a threat to intervene, would bring war with the Ottoman Empire.

During most of 1898 Crete was governed by the four Admirals and their modest militias, in regular touch with the Assembly's five-man executive committee (chaired by Sfakianakis), in uncomfortable cohabitation with the Ottoman governor and his army. This curious arrangement could not survive long. In a recrudescence of religious violence, in early September at the port city of Iraklio, several hundred Christians and 17 British soldiers were killed; Ottoman troops were implicated. Britain suddenly decided that things must change, and hastily espoused a recent Russian proposal, previously ignored, built on the foundation of the not-quite-forgotten Koundouros memorandum. Forgetting their concern for the Muslim minority, the four Powers found themselves pleasantly in agreement. Ottoman troops would leave Crete forthwith; the island would be ruled, under nominal Ottoman suzerainty, by a Christian High Commissioner, and for the next three years this would be Prince George, second son of King George of Greece.

THE GREEK MONARCHY
George I (reigned 1863–1913), born a Danish prince, was the best of the Greek monarchs. He guided the country for 50 years. He and his Russian wife Olga produced eight children including Constantine I or XII (reigned 1913–17 and 1920–2) and George (High Commissioner of Crete 1898–1906). Constantine married Sophie, sister of the German Kaiser Wilhelm II; their children included George II (reigned 1922–4 and 1935–47), the unlucky Alexander (reigned 1917–20), and Paul (reigned 1947–64). 'Constantine XII' was so called by way of claiming that the Byzantine Empire (whose last emperor, Constantine XI, was killed in 1453) was reborn in the modern Greek monarchy.

Venizelos's mother and brother, still at Milos, had died in the influenza epidemic of early 1898. Eleni brought Kyriakos and Sofoklis safely back to Crete when peace returned later in the year; another sister, the widowed Maria, came to keep house at Chalepa, where their neighbour turned out to be the Prince: he arrived at Souda in December and took as his palace the house next door to the Venizeli. Two days later Sfakianakis, Venizelos and three colleagues on the Executive Committee arrived for their first meeting with the High Commissioner of the new Cretan State. Prince George's memoirs recount at great length what he said on this occasion, omitting one remark which was afterwards widely reported: 'The blood of Peter the Great runs in my veins.'[2]

The first task, the Prince decided, was to draw up a constitution. He appointed Sfakianakis chairman of a 16-strong constitutional committee. Sfakianakis himself (his answer to the remark just quoted, 'I hope that your Highness will at least spare us the executions',[3] betrayed lack of appreciation of the Princely sense of humour) took little part and often gave up his place to the committee's Muslim vice-chairman. Venizelos, by contrast, was very active. What was to be the High Commissioner's title? 'Prince', said Venizelos: it was undeniably appropriate in this case and was quite commonly given to heads of state. It was agreed that the Prince was to have a five-man governing council, a cabinet in all but name. Venizelos proposed a bicameral legislature; then, since that idea was not popular, a single Assembly in which a proportion of members would be appointed by the Prince. This was finally agreed, the numbers to be 50 Christians, 14 Muslims and 10 appointed;[4] elections, as before, were to be held every two years. Guaranteeing representation to Muslims was not enough. In January the British Consul reported that the Prince's appointment had 'elated' Christians;[5] Muslim emigration gathered pace.

The debate over the High Commissioner's title had

unexpected ramifications. It led Venizelos to assert that Crete was entitled to its own ideas about its future, to which George retorted that foreign policy was not everyone's business, but that of the King of Greece and his government; he even characterised as 'traitors' any who insisted on calling him 'Prince of Crete' if his father decided otherwise.[6] Prince George was mistaken; it was not the King of Greece's business to lay down

> 'It is not everyone's business to conduct his own foreign policy, but that of the King and his responsible government.'
>
> PRINCE GEORGE OF CRETE TO VENIZELOS

foreign policy for Crete. The unnecessary argument foreshadowed bitter future disputes: between the Prince and Venizelos, between the Prince and the Powers, and between the Prince and the Greek government.

At the end of March the draft constitution was submitted to the four Powers, now represented as regards Crete by three ambassadors in Rome and the Italian Foreign Minister. The rebel Assembly's last act was to delegate 150 of its members to approve the constitution; it then dissolved itself, Prince George and his committee having agreed that until 1901 the governing Council should make legislation for a future Assembly to approve. He now appointed his first Council, including Venizelos (Justice), Foumis (Finance and Agriculture) and Koundouros (Home Affairs).

The next two years encompass one of the most intensive spells of hard work in Venizelos's career. Already prominent in the constitutional debates, he now drafted a swathe of the island's legislation, to be nodded through when the Assembly finally met in June 1901. *I once remained locked in the ministry for four consecutive days and nights without food or sleep*, he later recalled, *because I was hurrying to get the work done.*[7] The Prince meanwhile travelled the length and breadth of the island, encouraged the revival of the economy, started work on a monstrous government building on the edge of Chania, and founded what was essentially a new police force, the Cretan Gendarmerie, destined to play a significant role in Greek as well as Cretan history.

In October 1900 Prince George set out on a tour of the capital cities of the four Powers that still held the key to Crete's future. His self-appointed mission was to persuade them that the time had come to decree the union of Crete with Greece. His personal conviction that union was the only solution was reinforced by his filial and loyal desire to bring Crete into his father's kingdom; he was sure this could be made to happen through his close personal relations with European royalty. He never grasped what went wrong, though the facts are clear from his memoir, *The Cretan Drama*, which tells the story probably in much the same words in which he told it to his Council on his return. In March 1901 he had to report to them the Powers' final reply, newly delivered to him by the four Consuls: the Prince was warmly invited to undertake a second three-year term as High Commissioner, but union was impossible. The *status quo* must be maintained. 'They all shared my great disappointment except Venizelos, who said, … *It is the finger of destiny!*'[8]

What Venizelos meant by this oracular expression is clear to us, if not to the Prince. He saw that some external impulse, as yet unspecifiable, would be needed before the Powers would consent to union. The Prince's tour, like any other overt attempt to push them further than they cared to go, was a waste of time. For the present the best aim was enhanced autonomy. The nearer Crete came to the appearance of independence, the easier it would be eventually to exchange Ottoman suzerainty for union with Greece. Venizelos therefore urged that now was the right time to press for fuller autonomy. Crete had its prince, and the island could and should be recognised as an elective principality under Ottoman suzerainty, like Bulgaria. Crete was – Venizelos now repeated – *entitled to an opinion on a question which concerns its future*. Prince George had his answer ready. 'Crete has its own opinion on the matter. It has often expressed it, and its sole national aspiration is for union with Greece.'[9]

Venizelos's position was logical but impossible to defend. He published his views first in Crete, then in the Athens newspaper *Akropolis*. He was fiercely attacked in the King's mouthpiece *Patris* ('Fatherland') and in much of the rest of the Greek press. At least equally unpopular in Crete and now regarded by the Prince as disloyal, he offered to resign from the Council. The offer was refused; then on 31 March 1901 (on King George's personal advice to the Prince) he was dismissed. Immediately afterwards came the campaign for the Cretan State's first elected Assembly, in which Venizelos did badly, his group gaining no more than ten of the 64 available seats. His influence diminished further, soon afterwards, when the Council was cut to three members: it was his old friend and ally Kostis Foumis who was squeezed out.

The campaign and the Assembly session, which opened on 1 June 1901, marked the beginning of an island-wide season of demonstrations in favour of union, carefully orchestrated by the Prince. It had little effect on the four Consuls at whom it was aimed. They had been taken aback at Venizelos's electoral failure and for five more years their reports continued to exaggerate his popular support, partly because his views coincided with theirs, partly because their governments did not want to hear about pressure for union, and partly because of their growing distaste for the Prince's methods. Indeed, they were aware of being in the Princely firing line (the Italian Foreign Minister privately complained to the Greek Ambassador about a campaign in the Athens press 'against the Consuls in Crete, especially as conducted by the "official" newspaper *Patris*').[10] But the single most important target of the Prince's propaganda was Venizelos, who, having lost his political role, was now making his living as a lawyer once again, and for the third time in his life was publishing a weekly paper, *Kiryx* ('Herald'). The Prince's aide-de-camp, Andreas Papadiamantopoulos, was an accomplished propagandist, and to judge by immediate results he and the Prince had the best of it. Venizelos is said to have seriously considered emigrating to Egypt, and in March 1903 spent a few days in prison for a *Kiryx* article that described Metropolitan Evmenios (who had pronounced the Church's anathema on Venizelos as the Prince's opponent) as *an unworthy minister of the Lord*.[11] For the same offence *Kiryx* was banned for a month – the very month of the 1903 election campaign. In these elections the Venizelists won only four seats.

The Prince's victory came at great cost. From *de facto* head of state he had turned himself into a party leader, conducting a strenuous election campaign during which, by his own admission, he 'thought it was [his] duty, in touring the Island, to tell everybody to vote in such a way that ... Europe would understand that Crete unanimously favours Union. If on this account the Venizelist Party ... suffered defeat', he added, he was not to blame.[12] He had conquered hearts and minds in Crete; his father's court ensured a generally good press for him in Greece; but he had lost the ability to influence the governments of the Powers because he had alienated their consuls. Noticing that supposedly spontaneous demonstrations were in fact organised by the Prince, they deduced that popular opinion was against him. They discounted his election victories, gained, as they could not fail to see, with the help of improper influence both royal and religious. Since he complained spitefully about them in letters to their governments, they were ready to dismiss his campaign against Venizelos as equally spiteful.

As early as summer 1903 fears were expressed that the Prince's propaganda in favour of union could shake his own control of Crete. The then British Consul, musing over why Prince George pitted his 'popularity, prestige and royal birth' against Venizelos, concluded that the Prince had lavishly promised union, had failed to keep the promise, and needed a scapegoat.[13] A year later another Consul reported that Prince George himself was conscious of danger: he privately 'doubted whether he could continue to keep the people in check as he had done hitherto'.[14] Disillusionment with the Prince's relentless pressure for union with Greece led for the first time to discussion in the foreign press of the idea that a new head of the Cretan state, one who was not Greek, might manage things better.

By 1905 Venizelos's domestic life had changed. His wife Maria was dead, and Evanthia, now married with children of her own, took charge of Kyriakos and Sofoklis. He was often alone at home, which perhaps gave him more freedom of action when, in February, a so-called 'United Opposition' met at Chania to proclaim a descending series of carefully calculated demands: first, the obligatory union with Greece; failing that, modification of the autocratic regime; should that in turn not be possible without change at the top, the new head of state must be Greek. Venizelos was among the signatories, as were Foumis and a new collaborator, the wealthy poet and revolutionist Konstantinos Manos. The proclamation was aimed squarely at the four Consuls, who were certainly forewarned of it. They had several discussions with the signatories during the following month. Towards the end of March the French Consul was able to reassure Paris: 'According to my information, the [opposition] leaders are far from being activated by an impatient desire for Union'.[15]

Three days earlier, at 9 p.m. on 23 March 1905, Venizelos had left the Italian Consulate (almost opposite the 'palace') and leapt into the nearest cab – which, to his embarassment, turned out to be occupied by his sworn enemy Papadiamantopoulos. He hastily changed to another, and was driven along the carriage road to Mournies: that was as far as a cab could take him towards his destination. Fifteen kilometres south through fearsome gorges lay the naturally-fortified mountain redoubt of Theriso, his mother's birthplace, already famous in the annals of Cretan rebellion. Here the United Opposition had constituted itself a rebel assembly. Estimates of its number range from 600 to 7,000, clustering at the lower end of the range. The rebels proclaimed union again, raised the Greek flag again, demanded political change, and (with unusual moderation) promised to cooperate with the gendarmerie and the international troops.

This, Venizelos's second armed rebellion, was more peaceful and better financed than his first. As before, he kept closely in touch with the Consuls; there were few surprises, many friendly meetings. As before, it became evident that (in spite of their insignificant numbers) the revolutionaries were making policy, sidelining the island's established government. Elections were held in April, the Venizelists holding aloof; soon after, when the newly elected and unusually subdued Assembly adjourned in late June, many of its members quietly joined the rebels at Theriso. Even Manousos Koundouros threatened to take his supporters to the hills, in competition with Venizelos; the Prince himself, not to be left out, encouraged the formation of a 'popular militia'. With good reason, the remaining Muslim Cretans feared for their future. The Consuls' promise of protection failed to reassure them, and most of those still living in the Cretan countryside fled to the towns.

Crete was in a stalemate. Change came from outside, beginning with a traumatic switch of government in Greece. In June Prime Minister Theodoros Deligiannis (a fiery proponent of Greater Greece, unfriendly to the Theriso rebels) was assassinated; his successor, Dimitrios Rallis, took a fresh line, coldly instructing the Prince to disband his new militia, to carry out reforms demanded by the rebels and even to dismiss Papadiamantopoulos. Pressure on the rebels was meanwhile applied by the Consuls, who at last had to acknowledge that continuing chaos, supervised by rival armed bands, would guarantee economic ruin; but they were also convinced that rebel complaints about the Prince's autocracy had a basis in fact. A third external impulse was the weather: the White Mountains are cold in winter. Thus on 2 November Venizelos agreed an amnesty with the Consuls. A day later the Prince was told about it. Having taken three weeks to swallow this insult to his dignity, he proclaimed the amnesty; the rebels gave up their arms and returned to Chania as if nothing had changed.

Venizelos was not the real loser in this curiously low-key struggle. The Prince now submitted to the Consuls' 'administrative and economic control' and embraced an international Reform Commission whose evident purpose was to separate Crete from its current High Commissioner. Meanwhile the elections in May 1906 gave the Venizelists 33,279 votes, the most they had ever achieved, though still failing to equal the 38,127 gained by the Prince's party. In late July the Powers reacted to the Commission's findings in a Note. In two small steps towards union, mainland Greeks could now be appointed to the Gendarmerie and a promise was given that international troops would leave when stability was assured; but 'administrative control' was to continue, and the Prince, seeing his position as High Commissioner undermined, resigned.

It is hard to say who originally had the thought that the second head of the Cretan state must be a Greek. At any rate, in summer 1906 the four Powers recalled this idea and invited the King of Greece to nominate his son's successor. He chose an emollient former Prime Minister, Alexandros Zaimis, and the Venizelists were surely tempted to claim the credit, for here was the fulfilment of one of their demands of January 1905. Sensibly they kept quiet, fearing reprisals for the part they had played in getting rid of the Prince – who undoubtedly had the majority of Cretans on his side. Armed bands, led by Koundouros, threatened to keep him on the island by force. His hurried and undignified departure on 25 September 1906 was marked by violent mass protests directed at the Consulates.

Zaimis arrived a week later – *one of the better politicians of Greece; we all hope he will give the island freedom and justice and will guide it safely into the arms of mother Greece*, Venizelos wrote to Kyriakos and Sofoklis, who were now at boarding school in Iraklio. *I am sending you each a postcard with his photograph.*[16] Zaimis quietly set to work.

Venizelos was recalled as Councillor for Justice but was, as usual, short of money. He went back to his law practice, let the house in Chalepa (he was not to live there again until 1927) and took rooms in a big old house at the corner of Moschon and Theophanous streets in Chania. He was often not alone there. The death of a fellow-lawyer and friend, Athanasios Blum, freed Venizelos and Blum's widow Paraskevoula from the guilt of the attraction they had long felt for one another. She came to live with a relative, 50 metres away from Venizelos's rooms. Their nightly meetings did not go unobserved.[17]

ooooo

The Consuls and the Powers had, as always, hoped to maintain the *status quo* in Crete; not for Crete's sake, but because disturbances on the island would provoke instability in the Near East. They had failed. The upheavals in Crete in 1905 and 1906 were among the catalysts for a sequence of political shifts in neighbouring countries: Greece, the Ottoman Empire, Bulgaria, Bosnia and Herzegovina.

In Greece, royalty and conservatism had been made to look incompetent. In late 1906 a cross-party group of high-flying politicians pressed for reform – less for radical policies than for honesty and efficiency in public administration – and were dubbed 'the Japanese' in an allusion to the recent defeat of Russia by a newly efficient Japan. After two years in the spotlight the group collapsed when Dimitrios Gounaris, one of its leading lights, accepted the post of Finance Minister in 1908 under Prime Minister Georgios Theotokis. Like most would-be political reformers in Greece, 'the Japanese' achieved rather little. Yet no fewer than four of them, Gounaris, provincial journalist Emmanouil Repoulis, the radical educationalist Apostolos Alexandris, and – the eldest of the group – Stefanos Dragoumis, would later rise to prominence.

Prince George had quickly fallen from favour with the fickle Greek press. Athens looked afresh at Cretan personalities including Venizelos, who was noticed in 1907 when police chiefs from Greece came to Crete to advise on the Gendarmerie; and in 1908 when he was headhunted as a future leader of the Theotokis party in the Greek parliament. In government circles his readiness to work in step with Athens had not been forgotten.

The Ottoman Empire, bruised by an unending series of setbacks in its European territories and wounded close to its heart by savage guerilla warfare in which Greek and Bulgarian irregulars were fighting for Macedonia, had registered each new concession in Crete (a Greek as High Commissioner; Greeks in the Gendarmerie; phased withdrawal of international troops) as another humiliation. Now, in 1908, from their cradle in Salonica, the progressive Young Turks sent their ultimatum to Sultan Abdülhamid, the Empire's ageing ruler. Their original and basic demand was for a constitution (long ago granted by Abdülhamid himself, and immediately abrogated). But, logically, if the constitution were restored, minority rights need no longer be separately guaranteed; which meant that for the remaining Ottoman territories in Europe it was time to jump ship. First the principality of Bulgaria declared independence; one day later, Austria-Hungary announced its annexation of Bosnia and Herzegovina.

When Greeks and Cretans had looked for examples for Crete to follow, these were the territories that they had cited. Prime Minister Theotokis in Athens saw that the time was ripe. It is no coincidence that Zaimis, titular head of the Cretan State, had just left the island and was never to return to it; his work was done. It was surely after agreement between Zaimis, Theotokis and Venizelos that the next move was made. Two days after Bulgaria's announcement, Venizelos spoke to an ecstatic 15,000-strong crowd on the parade ground at Chania: *The Revolution remains peaceful and is*

*not directed against any power. Its sole object is the final
declaration of Union with the motherland. The Cretan Government will henceforth act in the name of the Kingdom of
Greece.*[18] The Cretan Assembly, summoned to extraordinary
session, ratified this momentous statement, and appointed a
governing 'executive committee' on which Venizelos held the
portfolios of Justice and Foreign Affairs.

Neither the Ottoman Empire nor the Powers were ready
with an immediate response. But the proclamation was uni-
lateral; it fell short of a formal declaration of union with
Greece, and Greece did not follow it up. *You did not move*,
said Venizelos to Theotokis later.[19] Many felt that an opportunity had been lost. Theotokis, who deserved much of the
credit for what had been achieved, was blamed for failing to
take the last step. In the pursuit of the Greater Greece that
so many Greeks continued to see as their country's primary
political aim, his moderation seemed weak. Domestic economic crises meanwhile shook his government. Ill-thought-
out attempts at reform alienated powerful interest groups, and
by spring 1909 it was not only the trade unions who were on
the streets. The army chafed under the cliquish leadership of
Prince Constantine, its commander-in-chief; what was worse,
non-commissioned officers now learned that new plans to
professionalise the army would block their road to promo-
tion. Protests spread. Revolution and republicanism were in
the air, and indecision gripped Parliament. Theotokis was
ready to resign; Rallis, opposition leader, hesitated to take his
place unless Parliament were dissolved. Everyone knew that
whenever Greece held elections the Cretans would unilater-
ally send deputies to Athens, and once they entered the Greek
parliament the Ottoman Empire would declare war.

The firebrand Theodoros Pangalos, at this date a mere first

3
Liberal Greece

In summer 1909 Greek politics reached boiling point. Crown Prince Constantine was discredited; the economy was on the point of collapse; there was widespread pressure for reform. Now, refusing to be cowed by the imprisonment of colleagues or by the arrest of their sympathiser Colonel Panagiotis Danglis, the young officers elected an administrative committee and became the 'Military League'. Naval lieutenants joined it; students formed a union in support. By 14 July the Athens daily *Chronos* was acting as the League's mouthpiece, and it can be no coincidence that at the beginning of the same month *Chronos* ran a write-in petition begging Venizelos to come and sort Greece out. Meanwhile Rallis finally formed a government, intended to last until April 1910, the latest permissible date for the next election, thus postponing as long as possible any provocation to the Ottoman Empire.

The last of the international forces left Crete on 26 July, Venizelos making an eloquent speech on their departure. Next day, in prominent positions throughout the island, the Cretan flag was replaced by the Greek. The Ottoman government at once protested, adding a complaint that Greek soldiers were fighting as irregulars in the bitter guerilla war in Macedonia. Greek ports were blockaded; throughout August war seemed imminent. Rallis's answer, that Greece had no involvement in Crete or Macedonia, was eventually, grudgingly, accepted; at home, though, it seemed like weakness. The arrival of British and Russian warships at Piraeus suggested that Turkish complaints had been taken seriously by the Powers; in Greek minds, however, the British vessels' presence was connected with a persistent rumour that the King was about to abdicate.

Finally on 28 August the Military League, assembling in force at Goudi near Athens, showed its hand. It demanded sweeping civil and military reforms and the dismissal of the Army's princely commander-in-chief. Constantine duly resigned. So did Rallis, to be replaced by the insignificant Kyriakoulis Mavromichalis, who accepted the League's terms and formed a government.

From his vantage-point in Chania, writing in his own weekly paper *Kiryx* on 8 September, Venizelos commented: *Obviously the King can do nothing better at this point than to hand over the throne to his Heir – because we refuse to believe that he has seriously thought of leaving Greece with his whole family, as is reported ... we refuse to believe that he considers not only himself but also his children, Greek born and bred as they are, so foreign to the nation that he can seriously envisage cutting the ties that bind the royal family to the Greek people.* Venizelos knew all about the demands that he should get involved in Greek politics; he knew that after his bitter quarrel with Prince George he might need to mend fences with Prince Constantine, who was no longer commander-in-chief but still heir to the throne. What Venizelos could not know was that on the very day he went to press in

Chania Constantine left Athens, to return no one knew when. Constitutional reform was addressed in a second article in the same issue of *Kiryx*. *If political decay ... has gone so far that the rebuilding work cannot be managed by the present parties and by normal means, the League of Officers must ... effect its programme by means of a temporary dictatorship (whose duration, of no more than a few months, will need to be determined in advance) and then call elections for a National Assembly to ratify the decisions already taken and decide how the state is to be governed in future.*[1]

Five weeks later the Military League invited Venizelos to come to Athens and advise. He replied that the League would have got further if it had worked from the start with a like-minded politician.[2] This was no flat refusal.

The League had by now realised that it would never complete its reform agenda through its stranglehold on the impotent Mavromichalis government, ready though this was to vote into law whatever bills, workable or unworkable, its masters cared to put before it. At a meeting of the administrative committee on 29 December Venizelos was proposed again, this time no longer as adviser but as government leader, and the proposal was approved with only one dissenting voice. The invitation was delivered by hand to Venizelos. He would agree only to discuss the situation. He sailed from Chania on 8 January 1910 – and again on 9 January, having encountered stormy weather – and met the League almost immediately on his arrival at Piraeus. He wanted no publicity, but his presence was widely reported and aroused feverish speculation.

He now dismissed the idea of a temporary dictatorship: instead, reforming legislation could be initiated by a caretaker government. He still insisted on the next step as prescribed in his *Kiryx* articles. The Greek Constitution had to be amended;

therefore, under the current 1864 constitution, a normal Parliament must be replaced by an Assembly (with twice the number of deputies). At Venizelos's persuasion the League soon saw that a National Assembly could be presented as its own crowning achievement. As to details, this Assembly might be Constitutive, if fundamental provisions including the monarchy were in question, or it might be Revisionist. Let it be Revisionist, said Venizelos firmly; let the King stay. Two important questions remained. Who was to lead the caretaker government after the imminent dismissal of Mavromichalis? Stefanos Dragoumis, doyen of 'the Japanese', said Venizelos. Dragoumis was not the League's choice (he had been too frank about them) but they submitted. And what was to happen in April, when, by constitutional rule, an election could no longer be postponed and Venizelos's fellow-Cretans stood ready to invade Parliament? An unconstitutional postponement, he replied, and he undertook to get agreement to this from across the political spectrum.

> 'The Assembly would be ready to vote for anything – including my own dethronement – recommended to them by M. Venizelos, who was now master of the situation.'
>
> KING GEORGE OF GREECE TO SIR FRANCIS ELLIOT

It required full use of his 'remarkable powers of persuasion'.[3] He, Dragoumis and the League agreed a list of ministers for the interim government. Meanwhile a Crown Council was held on 29 January. The King had had enough of the Military League and had ordered the royal yacht to be ready for departure, confiding to the British Ambassador, Sir Francis Elliot, his fears that an Assembly would be 'ready to vote for anything – including his own dethronement – which might be recommended to them by M. Venizelos, who was now master of the situation and was actuated by personal ambitions and by hostility to himself and the Royal Family, dating from the time of his quarrel with Prince George.'[4] Mavromichalis and Zaimis, who distrusted Venizelos, agreed. Eventually, however, the King listened to two other councillors, Theotokis and Rallis, current leaders of the two largest parties. Fresh from discussions with Venizelos, they favoured Dragoumis as caretaker; unlike Mavromichalis, they favoured an Assembly. No doubt they mentioned two fascinating facts: the League's promise to dissolve itself on the day the National Assembly was proclaimed; and Venizelos's insistence that the Assembly when it came should be merely Revisionist. This would leave the monarchy unshaken, and it also carried another implication. Delegates from beyond the borders of Greece need not be invited: the Ottoman Empire need not be outraged.[5]

The King acted immediately. Mavromichalis was dismissed. Dragoumis and his cabinet were sworn in and set to work, initiating major legislation whose benefits future governments would reap. Nothing was certain, however, until the dying Greek Parliament was invited to vote for its own replacement by an Assembly which would meet on 14 September. This vote required a 75 per cent majority; there were 150 in favour, 11 against.

And now, in a long discussion with *The Times* correspondent J D Bourchier, a friend since Theriso, Venizelos allowed his ambitions to show. He 'evidently means to take the helm by-and-by here,' Bourchier confided to his diary; ten days earlier a far-sighted *Times* leader predicted not the annexation of Crete by Greece 'but the annexation of the Greeks by the Cretans'.[6] We cannot say for certain when the thought of becoming a politician in Greece first entered Venizelos's mind, or when the idea was first spoken of by others; we know that

THE GREEK PRIME MINISTERS

Charilaos Trikoupis, once ambassador in London, served seven times as Premier between 1875 and 1895 (his father, Spyridon Trikoupis, Premier in 1833, wrote the classic history of the Greek War of Independence). In later years his chief rival was the nationalist Theodoros Deligiannis, who (having outlawed gambling dens) was assassinated by an obsessive gambler in 1905. Next the moderate Georgios Theotokis alternated in office with Dimitrios Rallis until Eleftherios Venizelos's arrival in 1910. In the following 40 years Greece had 40 Premiers. Among the most significant were:

Stefanos Dragoumis (1842–1923), son and grandson of politicians, Foreign Minister from 1886, eldest of the reformist 'Japanese' of 1906, Premier in early 1910. Of his sons, Filippos was foreign minister in 1952; Ion, a political writer, was exiled in 1917, murdered in 1920.

Alexandros Zaimis (1855–1936) son and grandson of Prime Ministers, served five times between 1897 and 1928. 'There's no fight in him: a serious defect in a statesman,' Ioannis Metaxas said to Venizelos.[8] He and Venizelos co-operated without warmth.

Dimitrios Gounaris (1866–1922), radical Royalist, another of the 'Japanese'; an overconfident Finance Minister in 1908; Premier in 1915 and 1921–2. When Venizelos returned to power in 1917 he was interned in Corsica; he escaped to Italy in 1918, returned to Greece in late 1920, and dominated the political scene. Executed in November 1922.

Themistoklis Sofoulis (1860–1949), archaeologist who turned to liberal politics; led the revolt of Samos against the Ottomans in 1912; rallied the island to the Provisional Government on 2 October 1916; Premier 1924 and after 1945.

Theodoros Pangalos (1878–1952), radical army officer; helped to bring Venizelos to Greece in 1910; backed Sofoulis at Samos in 1916; Premier in 1925, briefly dictator in 1926.

Nikolaos Plastiras (1883–1953), soldier, republican and Venizelist; led the revolution of 1922–3; opposed coup in 1927; joined unsuccessful coups in 1933 and 1935. As Premier after 1945 he worked with Sofoklis Venizelos for national reconciliation.

Alexandros Diomidis (1875–1950), academic and businessman, grandson of a prime minister, was Economic Minister under Venizelos 1912–15; special envoy of the Salonica government 1917; acting Foreign Minister 1919; Governor of the National Bank 1923; first Governor of the Bank of Greece 1929; Premier 1949.

Greece had its political families and patronage, but politics was not the road to wealth. Venizelos was a poor man until his second marriage; Trikoupis, Gounaris and Plastiras died penniless.

by early March 1910, when he returned to Chania, remaining doubts were being cast aside, and his correspondence with the influential Greek-Egyptian business leader Emmanouil Benakis, discussing the reform of Greek finances, was under way.[7] But his own finances needed careful thought. If he left his law practice and stood for the Greek parliament he would have no income. Kyriakos, after two years at the *gymnasion* at Chania, was now at university in Athens. Sofoklis was to leave the *gymnasion* in 1911. It must have been with enormous relief that Venizelos accepted Benakis's offer to pay for young Kyriakos to transfer to a Swiss university.

At all events, within a month Athens heard whispers of 'a new party pledged to principles of reform … No choice of a leader has yet been made, but … the name of M. Venezelo [*sic*] has been put forward'.[9] At the same moment Venizelos's popularity in Crete reached its modest peak; in new elections he gained a small majority, becoming chairman of the Executive Committee and, in May, President of the Assembly. It was a short and unproductive session, paralysed by Christian-Muslim disputes, eventually adjourned early in July. Seizing the moment, for the first time in his life Venizelos made a journey 'to Europe'. He went with Kyriakos to Lausanne to see the young man enrol at the Law School.

While he was away friends submitted his candidacy in the Attica-Boeotia list for the Greek National Assembly. His old antagonist Koundouros and his former ally Manos also stood. Furious at the manoeuvres over the Assembly, which were calculated to exclude Cretans, they got round the obstacle by standing for Greek constituencies. Although these elections were not quite enough to provoke the Empire to declare war, they were a sore point; the candidacy of Venizelos himself gave particular offence in Constantinople because he was so well known, and his career thus far proved him to be an Ottoman subject. It is true that, if his father held Greek citizenship, he too could claim it (in accordance with Law 391 of 1856; it was presumably on those grounds that his school certificate from Syros recorded him as Greek) but actual proof of his dual citizenship seems never to have emerged.

At the Greek polls Venizelos topped the list in spite of attempts to smear him as anti-royalist. The overall result was perplexing. The two main traditional parties had performed poorly during the months of crisis and were deeply unpopular. Both failed to make any electoral ground, achieving only 112 for Theotokis and 67 for Rallis. Against these stood a large and miscellaneous group of 146, consisting largely of new members (they had to be new, since the Assembly was twice the size of a normal Parliament), a good many of them independents with reforming agendas, some quite radical in their aims. About 80 of them were ready to form a new 'Liberal Party', which, they claimed, would not be a party of personalities like its rivals: 'a party of principles without principals' (as a sceptical newspaper jibed) already looking to the absent Venizelos as future leader.[10]

From Lausanne he sent a telegram to *Chronos* confirming that he would take up his seat.[11] Returning home by way of Rome and Athens he bid farewell to Crete and to Paraskevoula Blum. At the farewell banquet on 13 September, for perhaps the only time in his life, he was too emotional to speak.

On the crowded quayside at Piraeus, scene of many meetings, Venizelos was greeted by a delegation of newly elected deputies. His train was welcomed at Omonia ('Concord') Station, at the heart of modern Athens, by delegates of business associations. This triumphal entry into the Greek capital culminated in his still-famous speech from a balcony of the

Grand-Hôtel, where he had booked a twin-bedded room that he and his secretary, Klearchos Markantonakis, were to share. It was all he could afford.

To his left, raised a little above its surroundings, stood the Royal Palace; to his right, near at hand, the Hôtel d'Angleterre where he had debated with Joseph Chamberlain 25 years earlier. Before him in Syntagma ('Constitution') Square was a wildly enthusiastic crowd, primed with news of the Assembly's first riotous days. As had been noted by observers as early as April, it had the power to rebrand itself a Constitutive Assembly. The radical new party (still in want of a leader) pro-

> 'I do not come here as the chieftain of a new and ready-formed party. I come simply as a flag-bearer for new political ideas.'
> **VENIZELOS**

posed to do precisely this, and refused, in the meanwhile, to swear allegiance to King and Constitution.[12]

I do not come here as the chieftain of a new and ready-formed party, said Venizelos, well aware that a new and ready-formed party was already hailing him as its chieftain. *I come simply as a flag-bearer for new political ideas*; he would work with those whose views coincided with his own. He spoke of the monarchy's occasional weakness and of the impotence of the legal system: *Law turns out to be a spider's web, good at enveloping the weak, coolly thrust aside by the strong*; he spoke of the failure of personal politics and foreshadowed a new national party of reform with branch associations throughout Greece. He gave a little history of the League and his own intervention; in the course of this he carefully reminded his audience that he had proposed *a Revisionist Assembly* – at which there were calls of 'Constitutive! Constitutive!' – *I repeat, I gave the opinion that the Army should focus on the urgent task of restructuring the armed forces; at the same time I advised the League to demand, and if necessary impose, a Revisionist Assembly* – 'No! No!' the hecklers still objected; but this time others shouted them down – *a Revisionist Assembly,* Venizelos said for the third time, continuing as smoothly as if the flow of his sentence had not been interrupted.[13]

Next morning he voted with the Theotokis and Rallis parties, who carried the day against his own future supporters. The Assembly remained Revisionist and took the oath of allegiance forthwith. Dragoumis, commanding no majority, resigned, and it fell to the King to choose a new Prime Minister. Venizelos had the support not only of the newly baptised Liberals, but also of many independents. The public (or at least the press) expected him to be chosen. He was, and on 18 October he named his cabinet, star-studded but with little experience of government. It included two of 'the Japanese', Emmanouil Repoulis as Interior Minister and the radical Apostolos Alexandris as Minister of Education; also two former ambassadors, Lampros Koromilas to take charge of finance and Ioannis Gryparis, well known to Venizelos from his service long ago as Consul-General in Crete, now recalled from Constantinople to become Foreign Minister. A new Economic Ministry – assuming that the Assembly would vote to create it – was to be headed by Emmanouil Benakis. Although Benakis did not stay there long (he was elected mayor of Athens in 1914) he gave generous financial support to the Liberal Party throughout the decade, and his house in Athens was a centre of social life, focus for the alliance between merchants and Liberals. His successor at the Ministry, Alexandros Diomidis, was another wealthy businessman. In Venizelos's role as Minister of War he had a further appointment to make, that of an aide-de-camp: Ioannis Metaxas was to be publicly his liaison with the Army and privately with the King. Domestically, meanwhile, he had a hard decision to make. A financial subvention that he might have accepted as a member of Parliament he felt he must now, as Prime Minister, refuse. Kyriakos therefore left Lausanne at the end of his first term and returned to university at Athens. Sofoklis, to his father's relief, chose a different route. In November 1911 he was to be accepted (just possibly the path was smoothed for him) as one of the very small annual intake at the Officer Cadet School.

Venizelos had made his acceptance of office conditional on *freedom of action*, and it was widely assumed that the King had specifically agreed in advance to dissolve the unmanageable Assembly. The Theotokis and Rallis parties manoeuvred to avoid dissolution. When it came, they denounced it as chicanery and refused to stand in the new elections held on 11 December.

Venizelos's 1910–15 cabinets were quite new (none had served as ministers before). They included Alexandros Diomidis (see sidebar, page 38), Andreas Michalakopoulos (see Panel, page 90), Emmanouil Benakis (see page 130), and:

Emmanouil Repoulis, Albanian by descent, journalist, a 'Japanese' of 1906 (his colleague on *Akropolis*, Vlasis Gavriilidis, invented the term), radical; Minister of Internal Affairs 1910; acting Prime Minister 1919; shared Venizelos's exile 1920.

Apostolos Alexandris, proponent of demotic Greek, founder of Educational League; Minister of Education 1910; Ambassador to Switzerland 1918; Agriculture Minister 1931; spoke Venizelos's funeral oration in 1936.

Ioannis Gryparis, Consul at Chania 1889, Ambassador at Constantinople 1910 and 1912, Ambassador at Vienna 1917; Foreign Minister 1910.

This left a clear field for the Liberals, who had begun to found local branches (a new idea for Greece, championed by Venizelos in his Syntagma Square speech) and consulted local interest groups, such as business associations, in nominating candidates. They campaigned on a reform agenda. Venize-los travelled north with Metaxas and Alexandris to open the campaign at a mass rally at Larissa, almost within sight of the Turkish border, at the centre of a farming region still divided among large landowners. He spoke of the redistribu-tion of land, insisting that it would be a gradual and volun-tary process. As they returned towards Volos their train was brought to a juddering halt by an iron bar placed across the track. According to Alexandris, he fell on Venizelos and the short, fat Metaxas landed on top of both of them.[14]

The campaign was not derailed. As *Patris* put it, by their abstention the old parties had 'committed suicide to escape the guillotine':[15] the count revealed a Liberal landslide. They held 307 of the 362 seats in the new Assembly. It was an aston-ishing personal triumph for Venizelos, who had begun as an independent less than four months earlier and was now Prime Minister with a massive majority. The old parties never recov-ered from the blow. In retrospect the years 1909 to 1911 have been identified as Greece's bourgeois revolution,[16] or as the victory of the businessmen and the diaspora over the officers and bureaucrats;[17] the earliest victory of the new Greece of migration and urbanisation.

Venizelos held office without a break until March 1915. The second Revisionist Assembly was dissolved in December 1911 suddenly, because it became known that Cretans were on their way to join it. An election for a normal Parliament was held in March 1912; the Liberals kept their majority.

One aspect of the story of this five-year government is the catalogue of its reforms. Drawing on his earlier experiences in Crete, Venizelos now worked within a long-established con-stitutional framework and between entrenched opinions. His compromises, helping to make the revised 1911 Constitution a reality, bore on press freedom and on the language issue among others. Liberals demanded that the elitist classicizing Greek taught in schools, *katharevousa*, should no longer be Greece's national language. Within Greece people loved or hated it. Most Greeks beyond Greece's borders knew nothing of it; Venizelos, having attended Greek schools, was one of the few who did. He decided, disappointing many supporters, to allow *katharevousa* its place in the Constitution. That decided, however, the Ministry of Education, under Alexandris and then Ioannis Tsirimokos, was free to work with the radical Educational League on reforming the creaking school system and its syllabi. Everyday demotic Greek, *dimotiki*, began to find its way into the textbooks.

Some of the reforms of the 1910–15 government, insufficiently embedded, were afterwards revoked. Others stuck; economic reorganisation and agricultural advances set the scene for future prosperity. As befits the government's origin in a military 'revolution', its military reforms were among its immediate successes. No sooner had the Constitution been amended to permit foreign involvement in the armed forces than friendly governments were invited to advise. As already planned by Theotokis in 1909, a French mission arrived to steer the development of the Army. Venizelos had not made the choice, but (in conversation with Metaxas) he backed it on political and financial grounds: *Greek foreign interests compel us to turn to the Entente ... the French will also help us with the loan.* Meanwhile the retired and undistinguished Rear Admiral Tufnell led a British delegation to guide the development of the Greek fleet, and Venizelos gave pragmatic reasons for this choice too: *The Cretan question ... rests entirely in the hands of the English.*[18] Although Constantine and Metaxas, both German-trained, had argued forcefully for a German military mission, Constantine coolly acquiesced when appointed Inspector-General of the Armed Forces, a post very similar to the one he lost in 1909. By mid-1912 the standing Army had risen from 60,000 to 100,000 (135,000 on full mobilisation), and showed its capabilities in extensive manoeuvres in spring 1912.

The second half of the story of the 1910–15 government is that of its international relations, a topic bound up with the monarchy. The King of Greece had responsibility for foreign policy; in an arrangement championed by Metaxas, the Crown Prince was to command the Army when at war.[19] In early 1912 a military incident of pressing interest occurred at which Greece could only stand and watch. Italy made a surprise attack on two Ottoman territories, Libya and the Dodecanese. This latter consisted of Rhodes and 11 smaller islands in the south-east Aegean, whose Greek population greeted the Italians as liberators only to find that one foreign ruler had been exchanged for another.

Crete, too, remained out of reach. Germany had recently assured the Ottoman Empire that she would permit no change in the island's status, and Venizelos, at his first meeting with Kaiser Wilhelm II on Corfu in early May 1912, submitted to some teasing on the subject: 'As you cannot annex Crete,' the Kaiser said, 'the best way might be for Crete to annex you and send civil servants and army officers to conquer you.' *As you see, your Majesty, a start has been made*, Venizelos said with a smile. *I, the Prime Minister, am a Cretan.*[20] It was in the same month that Cretan deputies reached Athens with the intention of joining the new session of Parliament; Venizelos had to order that his own compatriots be forcibly excluded from the Chamber. If he had not, Greece would have been at war with the Empire.

But plans were maturing; Greece's frustrating weakness might soon be a thing of the past. Ever since autumn 1910 *The Times* correspondent J D Bourchier, based in Sofia, friend of Venizelos and of King George, had acted as intermediary in a slow Bulgarian-Greek rapprochement, the linchpin in a system of Balkan alliances. It was no coincidence that in 1912 Venizelos took an Easter holiday in the mountains with Bourchier (and the archaeologist Heinrich Schliemann). The final sessions in these sensitive talks were held – in loud voices, since Bourchier was deaf – on 17–20 April 1920 along the difficult footpath from Portaria, near Volos, across the ridge of Pelion to the spectacular mountain village of Zagora. The walkers were greeted on the hillsides with friendly rifle shots and on arrival were compelled to attend a lesson at Zagora's historic school.[21] Thus on 16 May Greece entered a formal alliance with Bulgaria, avoiding any commitment on how the spoils of a future war would be divided.[22]

Lampros Koromilas, formerly Finance Minister, now took over foreign affairs from Gryparis; the latter returned to Constantinople as Ambassador, but with new instructions. Having carefully noted the Ottoman collapse in face of Italian aggression, Bulgaria and her allies agreed in late summer that it was time to move. Greece had the congenial task of providing the provocation. During September all four states prepared for war, and there was close consultation between Venizelos and Prince Constantine. King George, having spent the summer abroad, returned on 5 October aboard the royal yacht *Amphitrite* and was met at sea by Venizelos, who had a hard task to persuade him that it was either necessary or desirable to provoke war with the Empire. At last, assured that his son had no misgivings, the King gave his consent.

The great day came on 14 October 1912. In Athens Parliament met and the Cretan deputies were formally admitted. In Constantinople Gryparis packed his bags. Three days later Greece was at war with Turkey, and 41 second-year officer cadets, including Sofoklis Venizelos, were promoted to sergeant and sent to the front. The network of alliances immediately brought Bulgaria, Serbia and Montenegro into the war alongside Greece. In this First Balkan War all four aimed to gain Ottoman territory; what was unclear was the extent to which their ambitions overlapped.

Somewhat to the surprise of observers the war was conducted efficiently by all the allies. The Bulgarian army advanced southwards on two fronts, in Eastern Thrace towards Constantinople and in eastern Macedonia towards Salonica. The Serbians pushed rapidly through northern Macedonia. Under the leadership of a newly promoted officer, Pavlos Koundouriotis, the Greek Navy set to work driving the Ottomans out of the Aegean. The Army, commanded by Constantine, made northwards from Thessaly into western Macedonia, aiming for Monastir. Salonica was a greater prize; both Greeks and Bulgarians desired it and a Greek physician serving in the Bulgarian army transmitted the secret intelligence that the Bulgarians were racing for the city. This was telegraphed to Koromilas and Venizelos, but Constantine, set on his successful northward course, hotly rejected the ministers' increasingly frantic requests to change course. At the last moment, the King – convinced by Venizelos that no time was to be lost – set out for the front in person and persuaded his son to turn east.[23] Thus the Greeks finally entered Salonica on 8 November, a few hours ahead of the Bulgarians. Venizelos sent a detachment of the Cretan Gendarmerie to establish order in the multilingual city.

By the end of November the Ottoman Empire had been expelled from much of its European territory. In the next two years well over 400,000 Muslims were to flee eastwards from these regions. Bulgaria, Serbia and Montenegro signed an armistice with the Empire on 3 December; the Greeks fought on.

Peace talks were held in London. As *The Times* put it, 'M. Venezelos, to whom the regeneration of Greece is so largely due, will come in person to uphold her cause.'[24] He arrived on 16 December, accompanied by Metaxas and others, and worked as much through personal contacts as through negotiation. These contacts were smoothed by the wealthy John Stavridi, Greek Consul-General in London and director of the Ionian Bank, and by two young women. Irene Noel, daughter of a British landowner in Euboea, wrote from Athens to put Venezelos in touch with Winston Churchill, First Lord of the Admiralty.[25] Dominiki Iliadi, an Anglo-Greek who had recently married the rich Liberal Lord Crosfield, arranged meetings with Crosfield's friend David Lloyd George, then Chancellor of the Exchequer. In Dominiki Crosfield's company Venezelos also encountered a wealthy heiress named Helena Schilizzi, whose family was well known in the London Greek community, and the attraction was sufficiently evident that, not long after his return to Athens, a newspaper was to announce their engagement. *They'll have to find someone else to bring those foreign dowries in,* Venezelos joked. *I'm not the man for the job.*[26]

At private meetings at 11 Downing Street Venezelos, Churchill and Lloyd George delved into the common interests of Greece and Britain, the potential for naval co-operation, and the future of two largely Greek-speaking territories that Greece coveted: Cyprus (a British protectorate) and the Dodecanese. A third important contact was Tache Ionescu,

Interior Minister of Romania. Ionescu and Venizelos, Anglo-philes, makers of Balkan alliances and riders of the middle-class wave in politics, became close friends.

At the Conference at St James's Palace, the Ottoman del-egation was reluctant to accept Greece's presence without a ceasefire, and persistently tried to make separate agreements to divide the allies. These tactics failed. The Empire finally gave up its long-maintained claims in Crete, which went to Greece. It prepared to give up Macedonia: northern Mac-edonia would go to Serbia, southeastern to Bulgaria, while Greece would take southwestern Macedonia and the great prize of Salonica. Bulgaria meanwhile would gain western Thrace. Still refusing to concede the eastern Aegean Islands and doggedly holding on in Epirus, the Ottoman government collapsed and the conference was broken off. The Greeks had been wise to fight on, securing Lesbos and Chios (Samos had gone its own way, declaring for Greece in November). Metaxas, Venizelos's aide-de-camp and a formidable tacti-cian, was hastily recalled from London to plot the capture of Ioannina in the northern mountains. Ioannina duly fell, and the army went on to occupy much of Epirus. Whenever negotiations recommenced, possession would be paramount.

January 1913 set the scene for a spectacular expansion of Greek territory, but little was yet decided. Greece still needed friends, and it was at this moment that Venizelos set up a press office (on the far-sighted advice of the junior diplomat Dimitrios Kaklamanos) to assist the many foreign corre-spondents who were in Athens to report the aftermath of the war. It was the nucleus of what eventually became an elabo-rate propaganda machine.

If one single incident in the First Balkan War can be said to have sparked the Second, it was the occupation of

Salonica. The Balkan allies had been able to unite when the territory they wanted was in Ottoman hands; they managed to remain united through the Conference. But in Salonica no ethnic group had a majority; the Sephardic Jews were the largest single community. Why should the city go to Greece by virtue of a few hours' possession? Greece meanwhile suffered a shattering blow when King George, strolling in the streets of Salonica on 18 March, was shot and killed by an anarchist. The King had ruled for almost exactly 50 years; for three of these he and Venizelos had worked together with increasing mutual respect. Constantine succeeded to the throne, aged 44.

The Greeks did not foresee a second Balkan war so soon after the first, but they knew it would come eventually; they knew the enemy must be Bulgaria, and their preparations were completed in time. First came an agreement with Bulgaria's northern neighbour. Romania had a special interest in Macedonia's minority population of about 400,000 Aromanians (Vlachs). In London Tache Ionescu had tried to reach an understanding with the Bulgarian delegate about guarantees for this minority and found him unsympathetic; Venizelos, however, when the subject arose, gladly gave assurances about minority rights for any Aromanians who might find themselves Greek subjects. In return, Ionescu assured him of Romania's friendly support should a dispute with Bulgaria arise.[27] Second came an alliance between Greece and Serbia, necessary to both because Bulgaria had ambitions in Serbian as well as Greek Macedonia. Venizelos hurried to Salonica, where on 1 June the alliance was sealed. One day earlier, representatives of the participants in the Conference had at last come together in London to sign the peace treaty; at that gathering the Greek-Serbian alliance was not mentioned.

Within four weeks Bulgarian troops had attacked Serbia and Greece along their new Macedonian borders. The two allies were ready with their response and quickly gained the upper hand. Greek forces, led by young Constantine, crossed southeastern Macedonia and were itching to march on the Bulgarian capital. Bulgaria now found herself invaded by Romania from the north; as early as 13 June the Greek Ambassador in Bucharest on Venizelos's behalf had asked Ionescu to be ready to move, and, faithful to his promise, Romania had mobilised as soon as hostilities began. The Ottoman Empire, not to be left out, invaded from the southeast. The Bulgarian government collapsed and King Ferdinand was forced to beg his neighbours for an armistice.

At the peace conference at Bucharest, which occupied a few days in early August, Venizelos once again represented Greece in person. All of Bulgaria's attackers gained from the war. Greece's gain was south-eastern Macedonia (awarded to Bulgaria at the London treaty only ten weeks earlier) including the major seaport of Kavala. All was not rosy, however. The frontier line was argued over bitterly; a line was at last fixed, but the Bulgarians felt they had been tricked and had given up too much.

Still, Bucharest was the culmination of what for Venizelos had been a spectacular year, one in which the land area of Greece under his political leadership had been increased by 68 per cent and its population by 80 per cent. As he returned in his first-class carriage from Bucharest to the Serbian capital Belgrade, from there through Serbian and Greek Macedonia to Salonica, and so to Athens, he might be forgiven for developing the feeling of satisfaction that he was to express at a celebration banquet given by the Liberal Party on 31 August. He told the story of how Constantine had hesitated to approve mobilisation, and how he himself had persuaded the King that Greece was well prepared. *'Sire,'* he had said, *'I guarantee that you will celebrate the fiftieth anniversary of your reign with a greatly enlarged Greece.' I knew that Greece would be enlarged,* he continued for the benefit of his audience; *I did not at that moment foresee that it would be doubled in size.*[28] It did not matter that this was an exaggeration; what rankled, surely, was that it discounted Constantine's contribution as Commander-in-Chief. On a visit to his wife's brother, Kaiser Wilhelm II, in Berlin a week later, Constantine was equally tactless. He gave the credit for Greece's gains in the Bucharest talks not to Venizelos but to a timely telegram from Wilhelm to King Carol of Romania; he attributed the Greek Army's victory to the 'principles of warfare that he and his officers had learned from the Prussian General Staff', overlooking the French military mission. This caused great offence in Paris; Panagiotis Danglis, Chief of the Greek General Staff, who was then at Aix-les-Bains, and Venizelos, who was taking the waters at Loutraki, both interrupted their cures to smooth over the incident with press interviews emphasising how useful the French advisers had been.[29]

In Greek politics Venizelos was sailing into uncharted waters. Already in March, with the old King's assassination, he had lost his royal liaison: Constantine had decided to appoint his old and close friend Ioannis Metaxas to the General Staff. The new link between Prime Minister and King was Giorgios Streit, a diplomat of German ancestry, who at the King's nomination was appointed Foreign Minister – an interloper in the cabinet. General Danglis himself, a Venizelos sympathiser, was to be another casualty of the new monarchy. Distrusted by Constantine, he was dismissed in November and replaced as Chief of the General Staff by

Leonidas Paraskevopoulos. Meanwhile Venizelos himself was on the way to becoming a father figure to people of the 'New Greece', the territories added to Greece under his government. He was one of them himself, a New Greek. This risked placing him in rivalry with the King, a father figure to all who served in the Army, a hero to 'Old Greece'.

Still, there was no quarrel. In mid-December the King and Venizelos stood together at the Firkas, the old Ottoman fortress of Chania, as the Greek flag was ceremonially raised to mark the longed-for union of Crete with Greece. It was the climax of Venizelos's island career; whatever rivalries might face him in Greece, he was now Crete's national hero. In many ways he would remain a Cretan all his life. In Athens and Paris he longed for proper Cretan food, wild asparagus, blanched salads of chicory and mustard greens and mountain herbs, olive oil – the real, unfiltered, biting olive oil of Crete – little Cretan olives, fresh mountain cheeses seeping butter, fresh figs, and the oranges of Mournies.

He stayed on in Chania for a few days, and his friends held a party in his honour. They sang *tragoudia tis tablas*, Cretan drinking songs. Toasts began, but the first speech was so emotional that Venizelos insisted: *We'll just have the songs and the laughter: no tear-jerking speeches*. Then Paraskevoula Blum appeared late – she had been preparing the sweets – and Venizelos broke his own rule with a toast to *the last-comers, who are not the least!* Their long friendship was never more public than on this occasion.[30]

4

The National Schism

Towards the end of 1913 Greece withdrew its troops from northern Epirus, which, in spite of violent opposition from local Greeks, was to join the new state of Albania. Uneasily conscious that Greece had reached its northern limit, Venizelos was convinced that the country still needed to expand; hence his widely-quoted comment to Repoulis as the Treaty of Bucharest was signed: *And now let us turn our eyes to the East.*[1]

Relations with the Ottoman Empire, which had never given up its claims to the Aegean islands, were soured by the dangers surrounding the millions of Christian Greeks who were still subjects of that Empire. Elated by recent events, they looked forward more confidently than ever to incorporation in a greater Greece; but the Turkish majority in Anatolia was learning national awareness, and found, in those same events, confirmation that Greeks and Turks were enemies. As was evident from the fate of the Armenians, the Ottoman government, far from protecting its minority subjects, preferred to give support and encouragement to their attackers; not least because, wherever Christian families were murdered or driven out, there was room to resettle refugee Muslim families from the Balkans. At times war seemed inevitable, but in summer 1914 Venizelos managed to soothe this deadly dispute temporarily by negotiating an agreement for the voluntary exchange of minorities between Greece and the Empire, with compensation for assets left behind, to be supervised by a joint commission. The arrangement was soon interrupted, but this novel idea set an important precedent.

The interruption resulted from ominous events in Europe. The shooting of the heir to Austria-Hungary, Archduke Franz Ferdinand, in Sarajevo had been the signal for warlike preparations among Austria's allies (the Central Powers, including Germany) and among the opposing Entente (Britain, France and Russia). Serbia's failure to hunt down the assassins raised the temperature.

Hostilities in Europe began five weeks after the assassination; but the First World War had already impinged on Greece. In late July Venizelos had set out for Brussels, where he hoped to meet Said Halim, Grand Vizier (Foreign Minister) of the Ottoman Empire, on neutral ground to forge an agreement on the still-unresolved issue of the Aegean islands. He reached Trieste by steamer, and there learned of Austria's ultimatum to Serbia. During his onward rail journey he decided on Greece's response, and from Munich he telegraphed Georgios Streit: since Serbia had provoked the conflict with Austria, Greece was not obliged by the 1913 treaty to take part. The gathering storm gave Said Halim the excuse he needed to cancel the meeting in Brussels, and Venizelos returned empty-handed from Munich.[2]

King Constantine now came under pressure from his wife's brother, Kaiser Wilhelm II, to bring Greece into alliance with Germany. On 4 August, in the course of a vigorous telegraphic

Greece must remain neutral and acted accordingly. But on 29 October, using the two warships, the Ottoman navy suddenly attacked Russian cities on the Black Sea coast: thus the Ottoman Empire joined the war on the German side. This immediately opened a gap between Constantine and his Prime Minister. Convinced that the Entente would win the war, Venizelos now argued that since the Ottoman Empire was a belligerent, Greece, its historic enemy, could not remain neutral and must join Britain and France, naval powers well placed to support her. The King, on the other hand, foresaw a German victory. Under intense personal pressure to join Germany, he had demurred with the promise that Greece would stay neutral; to break this promise would be dishonest and would open Greece to reprisals from Germany and a resurgent Ottoman Empire when they eventually won.

Now began a desultory series of discussions between Greek governments on one side, and Entente governments on the other, as to whether, and under what conditions, Greece should go to war. The King and his advisers still favoured neutrality, while successive Greek governments (led by Venizelos and others) faced mounting external pressure to join the Entente; Greece, therefore, was forever indecisive. The strategic aims of Britain and France were not identical, and Greece was not the only Balkan country on their minds; hence their responses to Greek enquiries were typically unsatisfactory and inconsistent. They, like Greece, were not sure how much they should commit to the support of Serbia. They, like Venizelos, at first doubted that the Ottoman government was solidly pro-German. They went on hoping, long after Greece had ceased to do so, that Bulgaria could be cajoled into an alliance. No wonder the discussions never came to anything.

For the first nine months of the war Venizelos directed

Greek politics unchallenged. Around December 1914 he and his Romanian ally Ionescu were speculating whether the Bulgarian danger could be neutralised if Romania and Serbia offered frontier concessions. Those countries could afford to make such an offer; Greece could not, or so Venizelos at first insisted. *Serbia and Romania can readily agree to cede Bulgarian populations, because … they are to be greatly enlarged in other directions by annexing Serbian and Romanian populations. If Greece ceded territory, however, she would either cede entirely Greek populations (including the Kavala district) or weaken her frontiers around Salonica. She can do neither, for the particular reason that she can expect no significant territorial gains. The millions of Greeks inhabiting Turkey are scattered… . Given that eventually they will be concentrated within the borders of the independent Kingdom, we must have space for them.*[6]

> 'The millions of Greeks inhabiting Turkey are scattered; given that eventually they will be concentrated within the borders of the independent Kingdom, we must have space for them.'
> **VENIZELOS TO TACHE IONESCU**

However, discussions with the British in January 1915 opened the question of 'most important territorial compensation' on offer in Asia Minor if Greece took the strategic risk of joining the Entente and giving military support to Serbia.[7] Though intentionally vague, the phrase was evidently a promise that Greek frontiers would be extended eastwards, at Turkish expense, when the war was won. This changed the equation. If Asia Minor were open to annexation – notably the region of Smyrna (modern İzmir) with its large Greek minority – the result would be a greatly enlarged Greece and fewer unredeemed Greeks. It would, therefore, make sense to go in with Serbia and Romania, and even to offer some territory as inducement to Bulgaria to join the alliance, if that would ensure an Entente victory.

In this way Venizelos completed a series of logical steps that were to guide his policy from now on. The collapse of the Ottoman Empire was the best hope for Greeks of the eastern Aegean islands and Asia Minor. If Germany lost the war, the Empire would collapse. If Greece were among the victors, she would share the spoils. Western Asia Minor would lie open to Greek annexation. Having already nearly doubled in size under his leadership, Greece could be doubled again![8] The prizes were prosperity for Greece and salvation for the Greeks of Asia Minor; but there might be other means to these ends. Some in Greece, including the charismatic thinker Ion Dragoumis, looked forward to a renewed Ottoman Empire animated by both Greek and Turkish cultures. King Constantine was not alone in believing that neutrality offered more to Greece than alignment with the Entente.

In pursuit of his vision, by early March Venizelos was making a new offer: for this promise of 'territorial compensation' the Greek navy would immediately support the Entente expedition to Gallipoli and the Greek army would provide a landing force 50,000 strong. At this point fantasy met reality. Metaxas, now Acting Chief of the General Staff, had already put forward a detailed plan for a Gallipoli expedition. Entente strategists never took it seriously. Metaxas, for his part, saw no good in the plan they adopted. It would not achieve its purpose; participation in it would weaken the Greek army, and whatever new territory Greece might eventually gain in Asia Minor would not be defensible. He would resign rather than lead the Army to Gallipoli under those terms. Venizelos regarded Metaxas's attitude as disloyal. He pressed his case at two Crown Councils, but the King sided with Metaxas, and on 6 March the government resigned. Dimitrios Gounaris accepted the King's invitation to head a government, and a new party gathered around him. He was welcomed by Vlasis Gavriilidis in *Akropolis* in words that briskly characterised the retiring Prime Minister and his triumphant rival: 'After the passion comes science. After haste, thought. After disorder, system.'⁹

A few months earlier, Tache Ionescu recalled, he had asked Venizelos the secret of his success. 'He replied that he had arrived at the right moment, and that he had adopted two rules of conduct: to tell his people the whole truth in all circumstances and to be ready to leave office at any moment without regret.'¹⁰ Venizelos now followed his own rule; after four and a half years in office, at Benakis's suggestion he took a holiday in Alexandria, where he was faced with a tumultuous public welcome and was comfortably hosted in the Benakis family house at the centre of the modern city. They talked politics. 'It seems we're not ready for democracy,' said Benakis's daughter, the writer Penelope Delta. Venizelos turned to her and asked: *Are you sure we're ready for monarchy?*¹¹

It was a good question. Gounaris's minority government, guided by science, system and Constantine, began dismissing soldiers and civil servants for supporting the wrong party, a custom that would poison Greek public life for decades. Otherwise it achieved nothing, and the elections called on 12 June stubbornly returned a majority for Venizelos's Liberals. Constantine used every excuse to delay summoning him to form a new government, and it was during this interlude that – in accordance with the King's consistent policy – new assurances were quietly given to Germany and Bulgaria that

Greece would remain neutral even if Bulgaria joined the Central Powers. Another event of this period, one that was not immediately known in Athens but would have far-reaching consequences for Greece, was the secret Treaty of London by which Italy became a clandestine ally of the Entente.

Venizelos finally returned to power on 23 August. Bulgaria mobilised and attacked Serbia exactly one month later, and this opened a second gap between King and Prime Minister: in accordance with *his* consistent policy, Venizelos immediately assured Britain and France that Greece would fight in support of Serbia. And so, in hasty response to Venizelos's equally hasty invitation, French and British forces under General Maurice Sarrail immediately began to disembark at Salonica, Greece's second city.

In Athens a showdown was inevitable. In words that have become famous the King maintained his constitutional right to guide Greece's foreign policy: 'When it is a question of foreign affairs … I am responsible before God.' [12] He agreed to mobilise the army but would not commit it to war. Venizelos went straight from the Palace to a private meeting with the British and French ambassadors. Then, after a fiery speech in the Chamber denouncing the King's *unconstitutional* position on foreign policy, he narrowly won a vote of

Italy was publicly a non-belligerent ally of the Central Powers; by the Treaty of London, on 26 April 1915, it secretly became an ally of Britain, France and Russia. Its new friends recognised its claims to the Dodecanese and to a protectorate over central Albania.

The Treaty was later extended by the Agreement of Saint-Jean-de-Maurienne in April 1917 which divided Anatolia into spheres of influence for Britain, France and Italy. The Italian sphere was to include the Smyrna region with its very large Greek minority. Owing to the change of government in Russia the Agreement was never ratified, but it still cast its shadow on Italian, British and French policy at the Paris Peace Conference.

confidence. Constantine would not give way, and dismissed him on 7 October.

The overt aim of the Salonica landing was to establish a base from which Serbia could be supported; but Serbia, having held out against Austria, was now caught by the Bulgarian pincer movement, and the Entente could do nothing to help. Unable even to get to Salonica, the remnants of the Serbian government and army made a forced march across the wintry mountains of Albania and reached Corfu, which was taken over by French and Italian troops as a sanctuary for them. A second aim of the occupation of Salonica was to force Greece into the war. Bulgaria's open alignment with the Central Powers had concentrated the minds of French and British strategists: Greece was suddenly the only neutral in the region; what was more, since Constantine was counted as a German sympathiser, there seemed a risk it would tilt the wrong way. If this happened the whole Near East would be lost to the Entente.

The actual effect of the landing was to split Greece. The Athens government, temporarily led by the emollient Zaimis, then by the aged Germanophile Stefanos Skouloudis, continued to clutch at neutrality; when on 16 October the British Foreign Secretary offered (without Cabinet approval) to cede Cyprus to Greece if it would enter the war, Zaimis politely declined. Elections were held in December; they were boycotted by the Liberals because under full mobilisation there could be no electoral freedom. Meanwhile Salonica was at war, *de facto*, on the side of the Entente, whose armies were recruiting volunteers and labourers from the city's hinterland.

Venizelos remained in Athens, in close touch with the British and French ambassadors and in contact with Liberals across the country. Abroad he was the Entente's best friend and Greece's best-known statesman; the first Venizelos biography, compiled by the journalist Konstantinos Kerofylas with discreet help from the Athens press office, appeared in Greek, French and English in the course of 1915. At home Venizelos's popularity was by now as polarised as Greece itself. In 'New Greece' – the territories which had become part of the country under his premiership – he was almost worshipped, as shown by his sweeping by-election victory at Mytilini (Lesbos) in May 1916. In Old Greece, and particularly in Athens, Venizelists were being purged from public employment and harassed by Royalists or Constantinists. These popular names for the Liberals and their opponents show that personal politics still flourished and that the King himself was turning into a party leader.

Neutrality was not to be had. Salonica and Corfu were held by the Entente. In Athens the British and French embassies openly favoured Venizelos, mere opposition leader though he was; their consular services refused visas to his political opponents; their intelligence organisations gave covert support to him and all possible hindrance to the Central Powers' friends and agents in Greece. With the help of their navies, they capriciously obstructed the movements of Greek merchant shipping. German and Austrian representatives were equally unscrupulous, if finally less effective. Then, with the Athens government's secret assent, German and Bulgarian armies occupied Fort Rupel, built by Greece in 1913 to guard the mountain pass north of Serres and thus defend the new border with Bulgaria. Eastern Macedonia lay open to invasion.

It was here, in the north, that change would eventually come. Already in early December 1915 Venizelos had heard of political stirrings in Macedonia that were to have momentous effects. The catalyst, perhaps, was a rumour that General Sarrail, commander of Entente forces at Salonica, intended to allow the King of Serbia to base himself there. Might the hard-won city be lost to Greece? The possibility was so disturbing that local Venizelists formed a committee, *Ethniki Amyna* ('National Defence'), whose aims were to save Salonica for Greece and to save Greece from itself by bringing the whole country into the war.

Six months later the Serbians had arrived and Salonica was no less Greek than before; but then came the occupation of Fort Rupel. Salonica was suddenly under direct threat from Bulgaria. Sarrail at once declared martial law, imposed military censorship and seized control of strategic points in the city. Meanwhile the French navy imposed a blockade on Greek international shipping, and Britain, France and Russia took three weeks to decide what to demand in return for lifting it. The justification had been the breach of Greek neutrality represented by the occupation of Fort Rupel, but it was difficult to argue this case while occupying Salonica. An early text of the ultimatum justified the occupation as having been undertaken at Venizelos's invitation, a claim that might well have ended his career abruptly. The British, French and Russian ambassadors rebelled against their governments and refused to present this text.[13] The eventual Note of 21 June accurately reflected the arguments of the Venizelists: since the previous election had taken place under full mobilisation 'the existing Chamber only represents a fractional part of the electorate'.[14] It lamely demanded the resignation of the Skouloudis government and the holding of new elections. Skouloudis instantaneously resigned, to be replaced by Zaimis.

It seemed that polarisation could not go further. Military reservists, demobilised and newly organised, ranged through the streets of Athens (the anti-Venizelists answering to Metaxas; the pro-Venizelists to Panagiotis Danglis, veteran of the 1909 Military League). There was wide acceptance, both in Athens and among Entente governments, of the proposition that either Venizelos or King Constantine must go.

Meanwhile in the northeast the Germans were advancing steadily from Fort Rupel (they were soon to reach Kavala); Italy, while no one was looking, expelled Greek troops from southern Albania, pressed on into northwestern Greece and occupied Ioannina.

The government's impotence was embarrassingly evident, and on 30 August *Ethniki Amyna* in Salonica made its move. Local administrative units (including the Cretan Gendarmerie, the city's police force) forswore their allegiance to Athens and placed themselves directly under Sarrail's orders. Venizelos already had plans to withdraw from Athens and base himself in Salonica, it seems. He was taken aback by this pre-emptive strike, but allowed himself to be reassured, and in the course of September completed his preparations in concert with two military allies. One was General Danglis; the other was Admiral Koundouriotis, hero of the Balkan wars.

Just before dawn on 26 September the die was cast.

The 'triumvirate' heading the Provisional Government at Salonica consisted of Venizelos, Danglis and Koundouriotis.

Panagiotis Danglis (1853–1924), Albanian by descent, was an artillery expert (joint inventor of the Schneider-Dangli gun). Chief of General Staff 1912; at London Peace Conference 1912; and War Minister under Venizelos 1915. He was acting leader of the Liberal Party during Venizelos's exile 1920–4.

Pavlos Koundouriotis (1855–1935), Rear Admiral, achieved naval victories in 1912 and 1913, and was a reluctant Navy Minister under Skouloudis in 1916. He was Regent after King Alexander's death in 1920, and President of the Greek Republic 1924–6 and 1926–9 (interrupted because he refused to preside over the Pangalos dictatorship).

Koundouriotis and Venizelos had dined late at the Plato restaurant at Faliro, Athens's second seaport. At 4 a.m. a French motor-boat arrived at the nearby jetty to ferry them to the steamer *Hesperia*; at Chania, which they reached that same afternoon, they proclaimed a Provisional Government of Greece, one that would embrace an alliance with the Entente. Danglis, having taken his own time to make his decision, applied at the British embassy for help in joining the others, but without success; it was again the French who ferried him to Chania on the 29th. The triumvirate called successively at Samos (which had declared for them in advance), Chios, Lesbos and Lemnos. They were welcomed as national heroes everywhere. But their destination was Salonica, where on 9 October General Sarrail, modestly and unofficially, joined the crowd that greeted them at the quayside. They dined in luxury at the Splendid-Palace Hotel, set up their Provisional Government of National Defence in the villa that had once been King Constantine's residence, and declared war on Germany and Bulgaria. As Venizelos explained it, *Greece can never progress, or even exist, as a free and independent state except by continued maintenance of the closest contact with the Powers that rule the Mediterranean.*[15]

> 'Greece can never progress, or even exist, as a free and independent state except by continued maintenance of the closest contact with the Powers that rule the Mediterranean.'
> **VENIZELOS AT SALONICA**

Seconded more or less openly by Entente forces, including the British embassy's intelligence service, the triumvirate established control of Macedonia, the eastern Aegean islands, the Cyclades, Crete and the Ionian islands. On the mainland the Entente created a narrow neutral zone separating this territory from that still governed from Athens, thus stifling the urge of Venizelos and his impatient partisans to move southwards by force. The Provisional Government governed largely by decree, but was radical in its internal policy. It at last made provision for the expropriation of large landholdings in Thessaly; its educational adviser Dimitris Glinos ruled that primary school textbooks must henceforth be written in demotic Greek, and both decrees were eventually ratified by the Greek Parliament. More divisively the Provisional Government awarded promotions for heroism to officers who had declared for Venizelos, putting them ahead of their Loyalist contemporaries and encouraging continuing defections of Athens troops to Salonica. By June 1917 the Provisional Government's army would number 60,000, Sofoklis Venizelos among them.

For the third time in his life Venizelos was in revolt. As usual he had acted in close consultation with foreign diplomats; the Salonica government now established its own international links. Its Foreign Minister was Nikolaos Politis, an academic turned diplomat who had already worked with Venizelos at London and Bucharest in 1912–13. Ronald Burrows, principal of King's College London, founder (in 1913) of the Anglo-Hellenic League and 'a devoted champion of Venizelos',[16] became the Provisional Government's representative in London, helped by 'honorary counsellor' John Stavridi and by Alexandros Diomidis, Economic Minister and financial backer of Venizelos's pre-war government, who commuted between Paris and London as special envoy. Venizelos himself made flying visits to London; Helena Schilizzi organised a relief mission in London (at 51, Upper Brook Street), gathering clothes and medicines, tents and trucks.[17] In the other direction Lord Granville, a career diplomat previously serving in Paris, was transferred to Salonica in December to represent Britain there.

Apostolos Alexandris, a former educational reformer, was Salonica's envoy to Italy, where his task was to encourage pro-Greek sentiments in the Italian press. It was a nearly impossible job: Italy, unlike other members of the Entente, regarded Greece as a natural enemy. Helped by Lampros Koromilas, now the Athens government's ambassador in Rome but more than half a Venizelist, Alexandris managed very well.

The principal aims of this diplomatic activity were to ensure that the Entente continued to favour Salonica and to encourage British and French propaganda against King Constantine ('Tino'; his family nickname became known from leaked letters between his wife and her brother the Kaiser). The most bizarre episode was the French Admiral Dartige du Fournet's demand to confiscate Greek heavy artillery and his armed expedition from Piraeus to Athens on 1 December 1916. This was a comic wild-goose chase in which the Admiral himself was briefly captured and chivalrously released, but its results were tragic. It led to 57 deaths among his own troops and, even more serious, to widespread attacks on Venizelists, seen by Royalist militias and their supporters as traitors in league with the Entente. Violence and looting continued for several days; at least 35 died; at least 900 were driven from their homes; prominent Venizelists were arrested, among them Benakis, the Mayor of Athens. These were *ta Noemvriana*, the 'events of November'. In territories governed by Athens the following winter and spring were cruel. A new and strict blockade was imposed. In the cities of Greece, always reliant on imports, shortages of food and medicines led to epidemics and to many more deaths. Theoklitos, Metropolitan of Athens, pronounced anathema on Venizelos for plotting against the King and the Fatherland, and 60,000 respectable Athenians waited in line to add a stone to the cairn that symbolised his excommunication.

In May 1917 London and Paris, both now under more decisive governments, decided to finish the job. The King must go; Venizelos must be reinstalled in Athens; Greece must join the alliance. Almost achieving the consistency that previously eluded them, Entente governments delegated their dealings with Athens to a High Commissioner, the French colonial administrator Charles Jonnart. On 11 June he presented an ultimatum to Zaimis, who was Prime Minister once more, demanding Constantine's abdication on the pretext that he had violated the Constitution of which Great Britain, France and Russia were guarantors. Constantine's eldest son, George, was also to be exiled; his second son, Alexander, aged 23, was to be allowed to take his father's place. Next day Constantine and his family left Athens for Switzerland. Georgios Streit, his faithful political adviser, went with him.

It was true that the Constitution had been violated; more serious violations were in store. Jonnart presented to Zaimis a list of anti-Venizelists who must be exiled. The most active were interned for the duration of the war on the French island of Corsica. These included the military leaders Viktor Dousmanis and Ioannis Metaxas, the former Prime Ministers Dimitrios Gounaris and Stefanos Dragoumis, and the latter's son, the writer Ion Dragoumis. Another recent Prime Minister, the Byzantinist scholar Spyridon Lambros, was among a larger group considered less dangerous and deported to various Aegean islands. He was to die in exile.

Memorably characterised by Lord Granville as 'the most orderly and conservative of revolutionaries',[18] Venizelos arrived off Piraeus on 21 June and sent for his colleagues of the Provisional Government to join him. But first he needed Zaimis out of office. Jonnart managed this by demanding the dissolution of the December 1915 Parliament and the recall of its predecessor, a demand that Zaimis was known to consider unconstitutional. Many years afterwards Venizelos admitted that *this enabled me not to hold elections, which at that time my government would have lost, given that ... the blockade following the 'events of November' had been used to poison the minds of the whole people against me.*[19]

Zaimis resigned. King Alexander, given no choice, invited Venizelos to replace him. The real balance of power was indicated by Venizelos's reported remark to the Russian Ambassador: *If the new King turns out not to be a constitutionalist, we'll deal with him the way you did in Russia.*[20] Venizelos afterwards thought it a mistake that during these political manoevres, and even while choosing his cabinet, he was on board the French fleet's flagship *La Justice*. When he entered Athens on 27 June peace was ensured by 'French bayonets'.

The June 1915 Parliament was duly revived. On 24 August, with anti-Venizelists in exile or refusing to attend, this 'Lazarus Chamber' gave him a unanimous vote of confidence. At a session two days later he spoke for over four hours, justifying his policies since the outbreak of the Balkan wars and the accession of King Constantine, vilifying political opponents and fence-sitters, explaining why (not for the first time) he *decided to become a rebel*, and concluding with bold promises concerning the future Peace Conference. *Greece knows that I have never promised her anything unattainable. Greece knows that I have never failed to keep my word. By taking part in this world war alongside democracies impelled to unite in a truly holy alliance ... we shall regain the national territories we have lost; we shall reassert our national honour; we shall effectively defend our national interests at the Peace Congress and secure our national future. We will be a worthy member of the family of free nations that the Congress will organise, and hand on to our children the Greece that past generations could only dream of.*[21]

Whatever effect this marathon speech had on its first delivery, it was to be highly effective as printed propaganda in several languages. The English version, *A Vindication of Greek National Policy 1912–1917*, eventually served as a main source for several biographies of Venizelos published in the early 1920s.

Venizelos's one overriding aim, from 1915 onwards, had been to commit Greece formally to war on the side of the Entente. He had finally achieved this: Reunited at last, Greece mobilised rapidly, and by late 1917 well over 100,000 men were committed, alongside Allied forces at Salonica, against the Germans and Bulgarians. Martial law was introduced throughout Greece; further deportations followed, and the freedom of the judiciary was limited; liberal newspapers appeared again; the Royalist press was censored. Stefanos Skouloudis, Prime Minister in 1915–16 and now aged 80, was charged with high treason and spent the next two years in prison. Officers who had served the Salonica government were given ten months of extra seniority, a cause of long-lasting resentment and jealousy. Patronage had always been present in the Greek armed forces, compromising discipline and hierarchy; under the 1917–20 government the tendency spread untrammelled. Even by sympathisers, such as his Salonica colleague

> 'We shall regain the national territories we have lost; we shall reassert our national honour; we shall defend our national interests at the Peace Congress and secure our national future.'
> **VENIZELOS IN 1917**

Panagiotis Danglis, now Commander-in-Chief, Venizelos was criticised for his failure to control his more enthusiastic subordinates. Discontent with Greek participation in the war and with forced mobilisation led to serious unrest in the Army, reaching a peak in February 1918, and to numerous executions for mutiny and desertion.

The country's near-bankruptcy brought pressing problems of food and military supplies, alleviated by Farming Minster and special envoy Andreas Michalakopoulos in long and exhausting negotiations in Western-European capitals. He and Venizelos worked with the Greek ambassadors, Koromilas in Rome, Athos Romanos in Paris, the aged Ioannis Gennadios and the young Dimitrios Kaklamanos, Venizelos's personal choice as attaché, in London. At the same time Michalakopoulos laid the foundations of an official propaganda machine and encouraged the Constantinople journalist Konstantinos Spanoudis to set up a parallel organisation among the 'unredeemed' Greeks, carefully insisting that they must appear independent of the Greek government.[22] Apostolos Alexandris was now posted as ambassador to Berne, the best possible location for keeping an eye on German and Austrian opinion.

Back in Greece a radical team at the Education Ministry pressed on with the reform agenda initiated by Alexandris and developed by the 1910–15 government and at Salonica. They encouraged teachers to re-think their approach; they created new textbooks, including an indispensable grammar of demotic Greek. 1920 was to see the foundation at Athens of a business school and a school of agriculture, both of which are now universities. *I consider our educational reforms to be the greatest claim to glory of my premiership and my greatest service to the motherland,* Venizelos asserted (to an educationalist, admittedly);[23] to the complaint that the ministry's leading policy-maker was a communist he retorted, *I am not interested in Mr Glinos's politics. I know that if I had a child I would entrust its education to him.*[24]

The British had more commercial weight and political influence in Greece than the French, and Venizelos was not alone in placing more trust in them. During the war, however – at least from 1916 onwards – France had led the way, Britain reluctantly following. France helped the triumvirate to reach Salonica. A French warship brought Venizelos back to Athens. France provoked every one of the major crises (the occupation of Salonica, the blockade, the landing at Piraeus, the expulsion of Constantine) that at last brought Venizelos to power and Greece into the war.

Thus it came about that at the Supreme War Council at Versailles in December 1917 Greece, now at last fighting alongside Britain and France, was represented by its Prime Minister. The new French Premier, Georges Clemenceau, presided; the British Premier, Lloyd George, played his usual active role. Venizelos's urgent pleas for food, military and financial support received a warm response: in this company he was regarded as his country's national hero. There were some in Greece who saw him in that light. Others, just as reasonably, saw Venizelist Greece as a satellite of the Entente and Venizelos as a traitor who owed his dictatorial power to foreign interference.

Until 1915 many Greeks could still believe in *ta dyo Vita: Venizelos, Vasilias* ('the two Vs, Venizelos and the King').[25] The public disagreements of that year had brought the latent rivalry into the open and trapped the protagonists in the polarisation of Greek politics, in which the King guided (and the Church supported) a conservative party; any liberal or progressive leader was therefore anti-Royalist, an anti-Christ, a traitor. Venizelos had triumphed, no doubt: he had defeated the King, driven opponents into exile and stifled the expression of dissenting views. He was left without any adequate means of counting his friends and enemies.

Venizelos at the Paris Peace Conference in 1919.

II
The Paris Peace Conference

5

Preparing for Paris

In 1917 and 1918, while Venizelos was steering Greece towards war, the war aims of the Allies had not stood still. During 1917 the United States associated itself with the Entente. Russia dropped out of the alliance and out of the war, abandoning any claim to Constantinople and the Dardanelles. Each member of the Entente was jockeying for its future position and keeping all possible options open. Perhaps Bulgaria could be persuaded to change sides, as Italy had done, if offered a little Greek and Serbian territory. As for the Ottoman Empire, it must almost certainly lose its non-Turkish-speaking territories in the Middle East; Asia Minor could well be carved up into zones of influence, as projected in London in 1915; the Empire's European foothold in Thrace and its control of the Dardanelles were attractive prizes; its capital city, Constantinople, geographically in Europe and with large non-Turkish minorities, was surely open to offers. Greece longed to play this game on an equal footing with its allies and might lay reasonable claim to Thrace, Constantinople, Smyrna and its Asiatic hinterland. Others also had claims, however. In 1917 Greece under Venizelos was a weak and debt-ridden state whose status in the alliance was probationary. She was often overlooked by the others, sometimes mistrusted, not uncommonly slighted.

Into this maelstrom of conflicting ambitions the United States gradually inserted war aims of its own and was well placed to insist on them, not only because of its economic strength but also because it was seen as standing aloof from territorial ambitions. With a view to the future Peace Conference President Wilson set out his Fourteen Points. Point Twelve acknowledged that 'the Dardanelles should be permanently opened as a free passage to the ships and commerce of all nations under international guarantees'. It also had a bearing on the position of the Greeks of Turkey: 'The other nationalities which are now under Turkish rule should be assured an undoubted security of life and an absolutely unmolested opportunity of autonomous development.' This left room to propose annexation by Greece as a means of assuring security and development to the 'Greek nationality' currently under Turkish rule.

In early April 1918, as the anniversary of Greek independence approached, the French and British governments assured Greece that there would be no inroads on her pre-war borders; Wilson joined this chorus with a promise that the integrity of Greece would be preserved in the peace negotiations. Thus assured, the Greek government began to work out its claims. Assuming that eastern Macedonia would be rescued from Bulgarian occupation, and that Greek possession of the large Aegean islands (never acknowledged by the Ottoman Empire) would be confirmed, these claims were to be as follows: northern Epirus (southern Albania) as occupied by Greece in 1913 and 1914; western Thrace, currently Bulgarian; eastern Thrace (excepting Constantinople), currently Ottoman; the Dodecanese, currently Italian; the region of Smyrna in Asia Minor, currently Ottoman. Greek interest in Cyprus would often be expressed informally but would not be put forward bluntly as a claim so as to avoid offending Britain, Greece's most reliable ally. On the question of Constantinople, Greece's usual ploy would be to encourage the idea of an international state of Constantinople (to be governed, most likely, by the Americans under a League of Nations mandate); if this could be achieved the city would in practice become Greek anyway.

Fortunately Greece's last-minute entry into the war had a decided impact. The Allied army at Salonica, after doing nothing for three years, moved forward at last. In May 1918 Sofoklis Venizelos was in the thick of the Battle of Skra, north of Salonica, which first demonstrated the potential of the newly-reinforced expeditionary troops. it. In the late summer the Bulgarians were driven into retreat; on 29 September 1918 they capitulated, the first among the Central Powers to do so. The terms of the armistice required Greece to re-occupy eastern Macedonia at once, thus wiping out the bitter memory of Fort Rupel. Having got so far, the Greeks wanted to go on winning. The one enemy still within reach was the Ottoman Empire. There was some prospect – if peace did not come too soon – of a rapid march on Constantinople, and of a landing at Smyrna as preliminary to an invasion of Asia Minor, in both of which Greek troops might share and from which Greece might gain. As the re-occupation of eastern Macedonia got under way, British, French and Italian policy-makers met at Versailles to decide how to finish with the Ottoman Empire. Ambassador Romanos urged Venizelos to get there at once: 'Lloyd George has just told me that the Italians have again insisted on their claims in Asia Minor and

PRESIDENT WILSON'S FOURTEEN POINTS, 8 JANUARY 1918

The program of the world's peace, therefore, is our program; and that program, the only possible program, as we see it, is this:

I. Open covenants of peace, openly arrived at, after which there shall be no private international understandings of any kind but diplomacy shall proceed always frankly and in the public view.

II. Absolute freedom of navigation upon the seas, outside territorial waters, alike in peace and in war, except as the seas may be closed in whole or in part by international action for the enforcement of international covenants.

III. The removal, so far as possible, of all economic barriers and the establishment of an equality of trade conditions among all the nations consenting to the peace and associating themselves for its maintenance.

IV. Adequate guarantees given and taken that national armaments will be reduced to the lowest point consistent with domestic safety.

V. A free, open-minded, and absolutely impartial adjustment of all colonial claims, based upon a strict observance of the principle that in determining all such questions of sovereignty the interests of the populations concerned must have equal weight with the equitable claims of the government whose title is to be determined.

VI. The evacuation of all Russian territory and such a settlement of all questions affecting Russia as will secure the best and freest cooperation of the other nations of the world in obtaining for her an unhampered and unembarrassed opportunity for the independent determination of her own political development and national policy and assure her of a sincere welcome into the society of free nations under institutions of her own choosing; and, more than a welcome, assistance also of every kind that she may need and may herself desire. The treatment accorded Russia by her sister nations in the months to come will be the acid test of their good will, of their comprehension of her needs as distinguished from their own interests, and of their intelligent and unselfish sympathy.

VII. Belgium, the whole world will agree, must be evacuated and restored, without any attempt to limit the sovereignty which she enjoys in common with all other free nations. No other single act will serve as this will serve to restore confidence among the nations in the laws which they have themselves set and determined for the government of their relations with one another. Without this healing act the whole structure and validity of international law is forever impaired.

VIII. All French territory should be freed and the invaded portions restored, and the wrong done to France by Prussia in 1871 in the matter of Alsace-Lorraine, which has unsettled the peace of the world for nearly fifty years, should be righted, in order that peace may once more be made secure in the interest of all.

IX. A readjustment of the frontiers of Italy should be effected along clearly recognizable lines of nationality.

X. The peoples of Austria-Hungary, whose place among the nations we wish to see safeguarded and assured, should be accorded the freest opportunity to autonomous development.

XI. Rumania, Serbia, and Montenegro should be evacuated; occupied territories restored; Serbia accorded free and secure access to the sea; and the relations of the several Balkan states to one another determined by friendly counsel along historically established lines of allegiance and nationality; and international guarantees of the political and economic independence and territorial integrity of the several Balkan states should be entered into.

XII. The Turkish portion of the present Ottoman Empire should be assured a secure sovereignty, but the other nationalities which are now under Turkish rule should be assured an undoubted security of life and an absolutely unmolested opportunity of autonomous development, and the Dardanelles should be permanently opened as a free passage to the ships and commerce of all nations under international guarantees.

XIII. An independent Polish state should be erected which should include the territories inhabited by indisputably Polish populations, which should be assured a free and secure access to the sea, and whose political and economic independence and territorial integrity should be guaranteed by international covenant.

XIV. A general association of nations must be formed under specific covenants for the purpose of affording mutual guarantees of political independence and territorial integrity to great and small states alike.

the Aegean Islands, claims that are very damaging to Greece;' what was more, if one were going for a separate peace, 'probably one could not ask Turkey to cede Smyrna'.[1] Venizelos dropped everything and set out on 9 October. It was time to begin fighting the peace.

He arrived at the Gare de Lyon on the morning of the 12th to find that the peacemakers had gone. They had decided to make no separate peace with Turkey after all: Clemenceau had been against it. After a day of meetings Venizelos made for the Gare du Nord and travelled overnight to London. On 15 October he had an informal lunch with Lloyd George. They talked about Asia Minor, where, assuming it remained part of a Turkish state, minorities might be protected by international supervision. Venizelos expressed doubt whether Albania could survive as an independent state; especially if it were to become an Italian protectorate, he urged that Greece should have southern Epirus. In spite of strongly expressed Italian opposition, Lloyd George appeared to favour Greek participation in any future military operations in the Ottoman Empire.[2]

Towards the end of October Venizelos returned to Paris, where the Supreme War Council of the Entente, luxuriously settled at the Trianon Palace Hotel in Versailles, was about to discuss armistice terms. He had been urged to think of a visit to Washington so as to get to know President Wilson before the Peace Conference began. As a start, on 27 October he renewed his acquaintance with 'Colonel' Edward House, Wilson's usual representative at the Supreme War Council. House hinted that he himself was Washington's policy-maker and that crossing the Atlantic would be a waste of time. The idea was dropped. Since Wilson's Four Principles emphasised national self-determination, Venizelos needed an ethnographic map of south-eastern Europe and Asia Minor designed to support the Greek case. Kaklamanos, attaché at the London embassy, arranged with Stanford's to print and publish it. In Paris, on the same day on which he met House, Venizelos studied a draft of the map and corrected numerous details. It was ready for distribution before the Conference, as a stand-alone map and in a booklet published by the Anglo-Hellenic League; on 1 March 1919 it would be given mass circulation as a paid supplement to the illustrated London weekly *Sphere*. Supporting evidence to back the claims in Asia Minor was also wanted urgently. Leon Makkas, Greek journalist and propagandist in Paris, was commissioned at the last possible moment to produce a text, *L'hellénisme en Asie Mineur: son historie, sa puissance, son sort*. He had it ready for distribution in mid December.

The sudden emphasis on self-determination led Foreign Minister Politis, back in Athens, to telegraph a suggestion that the Peace Conference must be addressed directly by the Greeks of Turkey. Venizelos acted immediately, asking Michalakopoulos's contact in London, the journalist Spanoudis, to set up shop in Paris. As a result, a 'congress' assembled during November (from Britain and France, with a few representatives from the United States, Greece and Egypt; but there was not a single one from Turkey). A five-member Council was elected, and in 1919 this became the official Delegation of Unredeemed Greeks. As Michalakopoulos observed, 'politicians and journalists never ask a Committee of this kind whether it really has a mandate'.[3]

During these few days in Paris Venizelos wrote a memorandum on the future of the Ottoman Empire for Lloyd George. Assuming that British and French plans to detach Syria, Palestine, Iraq and Arabia would take effect, he dealt only with the remainder. He proposed an Armenian state in the east, a Turkish state in the centre of the peninsula, and a western region centred on Smyrna to be annexed by Greece. This region would, he calculated, have a population of 1.6 million, divided about equally between Greeks and Muslims. The Muslims should be encouraged to migrate to the Turkish state; a roughly equal number of Greeks, inhabiting scattered districts of the Turkish state, would similarly migrate to Asiatic Greece. In a private letter to Lloyd George he urged that the Greek claim to Asia Minor, unlike the competing Italian claim, was in accord with the principles of self-determination; it would be quite unreasonable, when Serbia and Romania were to expand to meet national aspirations, to leave so many Greeks outside the borders of Greece.[4]

He was soon in London again. The moment of victory over Germany was a fitting time to accept the resignation of the venerable Greek ambassador Ioannis Gennadios, who had served in London since 1876 and had been fiercely obstructive in his dealings with Michalakopoulos and the young propagandist Kaklamanos. Gennadios became 'honorary Minister' and Kaklamanos took his place. But Venizelos's main purpose was to confer once again with his long-standing Balkan allies, the Serbian Nikola Pašić and the Romanian Tache Ionescu; the latter had been in Paris since the summer, heading a propaganda mission which was soon to be supplanted by the official Romanian delegation. On 21 November the three together submitted a joint memorandum to the Foreign Office that announced an embryonic alliance. The three states would maintain a close and cordial union and would abide by the principle of nationality; to Bulgaria they offered 'justice' but not alliance. The national principle, as the three allies interpreted it, would allocate eastern and western Thrace to Greece.[5]

Towards the end of November, for the last time on this exhausting sojourn in the West, Venizelos returned to Paris. Long ago he had met, and impressed, Clemenceau when the Frenchman visited Crete in 1899. They now agreed that Greek troops would take part in the expedition to the Ukraine, then being mounted by France with the aim of supporting anti-Communist resistance in Russia. This offer was a valuable one and Clemenceau was willing to bargain. He agreed that at the future Peace Conference he would support Greek claims to Thrace, but not to Smyrna unless the British or Americans made the suggestion first.[6]

However hopeful Venizelos might feel as he returned to Athens for a short breathing-space, no gains were guaranteed. Greece would face powerful opposition. During these few days he had to play down a possible enlargement, damping the speculation that was rife in the Greek newspapers.

The time to set out for the Peace Conference had arrived, and Greece was to be entrusted for several months to other hands. Venizelos remained Prime Minister but he would be representing Greece in Paris; Emmanouil Repoulis, for most of the last ten years a minister in Venizelist governments, was to be Deputy Prime Minister. Nikolaos Politis, a learned and effective Foreign Minister, took second place in the Peace Conference delegation; his deputy at home was to be Alexandros Diomidis.

The delegation was remarkably high-powered, headed as it was by three serving cabinet ministers, supported by the serving ambassadors to Paris and Rome. Yet it was something of an extended family, including three members of the Politis family and three Venizeli. Kyriakos, Venizelos's elder son, currently a secretary at the Greek embassy in Paris, was to join the secretariat. His brother Sofoklis, now holding the rank of captain, served as his father's aide-de-camp and message boy. On Boxing Day it would be Sofoklis' turn to be sent to London carrying a propaganda film for Kaklamanos to distribute.

Thus, on 7 December, Venizelos set out westwards once more, this time travelling with Politis and the rest of the delegation, accompanied by Commander Gerald Talbot, the newly appointed British naval attaché whose real duty turned out to be to act as liaison between Greeks and British in Paris. Their steamer took them by way of Corfu to Taranto, where a special train waited to carry them on to Rome. Two railway workers were killed by this train; the unlucky incident was a gift to the Italian press, as fervently anti-Greek as the Greek press was anti-Italian.

The delegation spent two days in Rome; a holiday for some, but Venizelos and Politis engaged in unproductive talks with the Italian Prime Minister, Vittorio Orlando, and his Foreign Minister, Sidney Sonnino. Italy and Greece were natural rivals for power and influence in the Mediterranean. The rivalry was intensified by public opinion. Both peoples had needed persuasion to acquiesce in joining the Entente; they expected victory to bring territorial gains. At the Peace Conference Italy's claims were bound to conflict with those of Greece. Italy occupied much of Albania (and even an adjacent sliver of Greece). As agreed at London and Saint-Jean-de-Maurienne (see sidebar, p 62) it expected to retain the Greek-speaking Dodecanese and to gain south-western Anatolia as her sphere of influence, including the Smyrna region coveted by Greece.

Both the Greek and the Italian governments risked electoral failure if they failed to meet popular expectations. Britain and France, conscious of having given too much away in those wartime agreements, were more sympathetic to Greece than to Italy; the Italians knew it, and found their interests threatened by Wilson's rejection of the agreements and by his firmly-stated principles (to which they had already tried to urge adjustments in their own favour). Venizelos probably did not realise how panicky the Italians were.

He spoke to Orlando on the first day, suggesting that while Asia Minor was a complicated issue because of British and French interests, it might be possible for Greece and Italy to reach some informal agreement on northern Epirus and the Dodecanese before the Conference began. Orlando warned him that Sonnino would not be easy to persuade. Next day, mutual mistrust and conflicting negotiating styles halted the discussions at the Foreign Ministry before they began. Venizelos raised the issue of the Dodecanese, islands whose population was almost wholly Greek; would Italy consider giving them up? Sonnino responded with what was intended as a put-down. Cyprus likewise had a large Greek majority; why didn't Venizelos ask Britain to give up Cyprus? To Sonnino's discomfiture, Venizelos was able to turn the question round. Yes, in fact, Britain was considering ceding Cyprus; if she did so, would Italy then cede the Dodecanese? This was a clever but useless argument. Sonnino simply fell back on his initial position: northern Epirus and the Dodecanese would be discussed in Paris. All that was achieved was to convince Venizelos that he must make friends with the Americans, who might hold the balance. Their precise views were as yet unknown. It was true that President Wilson favoured Bulgaria and had described as unjust the 1913 Treaty of Bucharest, which confiscated so much territory from Bulgaria; yet in general the American principles and points seemed to favour Greek claims rather than Italian.

THE GREEK DELEGATION

Venizelos dominated the Greek government delegation at Paris. Other heavyweights were:

Lampros Koromilas (1856–1923), oldest of the party. As consul at Salonica in 1904 he secretly co-ordinated the guerilla war in Macedonia. He was Venizelos's Economic Minister 1910, Foreign Minister 1912; Ambassador to Italy 1913–20, recalled for protesting at the Asia Minor adventure.

Athos Romanos (1858–1940), Foreign Minister soon after 1900, then diplomat. He represented Greece at Edward VII's funeral in 1910; by 1919 he was the serving Greek ambassador at Paris. In 1935–6 he helped to mend fences between Venizelos and King George II.

Nikolaos Politis (1872–1942) gave up his academic career in foreign affairs to be Venizelos's Foreign Minister at Salonica, 1916–17, and at Athens, 1917–20. He represented Greece at the League of Nations, 1920–24.

Andreas Michalakopoulos (1875–1938) was one of Venizelos's most faithful collaborators: Minister for National Economy 1912; Agriculture Minister at Salonica and then Athens; Minister without Portfolio and special envoy in western Europe 1918. In the mid-1920s he led one of the Venizelist parties and was Prime Minister 1924–5. He was Foreign Minister for most of the period 1926–33.

The Greek party included three serving cabinet ministers (Venizelos, Politis and Michalakopoulos), three future Prime Ministers (Michalakopoulos, Emmanouil Tsouderos[7] and Sofoklis Venizelos) and a very young future President of Greece (Konstantinos Tsatsos).

Aside from the government delegation, the Délégation des Grecs Irrédimés was led by Konstantinos Spanoudis. The Greeks of Thrace were headed by Ch. Vamvakas. Pontic Greeks were represented by Metropolitan Chrysanthos. The Delegation of the Dodecanese was led by Skevos Zervos. Four northern Epirus delegates were led by Alexandros Karapanos, a leading figure in the revolutionary government of Northern Epirus that held the ring between the Greek occupation of 1913 and that of 1914; he was Foreign Minister under Venizelos in 1928–9.

The Greek delegation reached Paris on the morning of 12 December. Romanos had tried to rent a large house for them but failed to find anything suitable. He settled for three floors of the Hôtel Mercédès, a solid, almost-new structure, ideally located on the narrow rue de Presbourg encircling the place de l'Etoile.

From now on it was Politis who worked with the propagandists, centred at the newly-established Bureau d'Information Hellénique at 25, rue de Bassano, just ten minutes' walk from the Mercédès. Greece had plenty of friends among the journalists at Paris, notably Wickham Steed, foreign editor and from February 1919 editor of the *Times*, a Bulgarophile turned Hellenophile. Emile Joseph Dillon, a *Daily Telegraph* correspondent, had made the introduction (at Claridge's in January 1913) between Venizelos and his first biographer, Konstantinos Kerofylas; Dillon was planning a book about the Conference and was soon to write a life of Venizelos.

Politis also acted as primary contact with the delegations of 'unredeemed' Greeks. The northern Epirus delegates lived in state at the Grand-Hôtel near the Opéra. The Delegation of the Dodecanese stayed modestly in an apartment at 4, avenue de Messine: they were to play a crucial role. Others clustered at the Hôtel Campbell, 47, avenue Friedland, and among them was Metropolitan Chrysanthos of Trebizond, 'a splendid if turbulent priest',[8] who went to work ambitiously in Paris and London on behalf of the Greeks of the Pontus (northern Anatolia). He got nothing from Venizelos, who never seriously considered asking either for the Pontus to be attached to Greece (which would create an indefensible frontier) or for a Pontic-Armenian federation (because the Pontic Greeks were too thinly scattered). His solution was to incorporate a limited Greek-speaking nucleus of the Pontus in the independent Armenian state. *I give you Trebizond*, he said to the Armenian delegates at a private meeting. *You need a seaport. The friendship between Greeks and Armenians has lasted a millennium, and my gesture will strengthen it ... Once free to fix their own destiny, Greeks and Armenians will live as brothers and will spread their civilization across Asia Minor for the good of all its peoples.*[9] It came to nothing: independent Armenia was to be one of the unrealised fantasies of the Peace Conference.

A delegation of Greek Cypriots was in London throughout 1919. They had a dusty reception from the British government and never saw Lloyd George. From Venizelos they got scarcely a message. Politis and Kaklamanos, acting on his instructions, gave them frequent soothing advice and strongly discouraged them from coming to Paris. Venizelos hoped that Britain would transfer Cyprus (the idea was in Lloyd George's mind) but he saw that pressure from the Greeks of the island would be a hindrance rather than a help. There was powerful opposition to the transfer. Writing in early 1919 Lord Milner, British Colonial Secretary and imperialist, made an interesting distinction between ethnicity and language: 'Cyprus has never in all its history been part of Greece and there is absolutely no case for Greece having it, except that there is a decided majority of Greeks, or at any rate Greek speaking people.'[10]

The British were living at the massive Majestic Hôtel, 19, avenue Kléber, only a few yards from the Mercédès, which they would pass on the way to their offices (these were at the Astoria on the avenue des Champs-Elysées). Not far off, Lloyd George and his Foreign Secretary, Arthur Balfour, enjoyed their freedom in two modest but comfortable flats at 23, rue Nitot. A cab-ride away from this diplomatic ghetto – and just across the river from the Quai d'Orsay, the French Foreign Ministry – the Americans settled at the magnificent Hôtel de Crillon on the place de la Concorde, a neoclassical structure that put at least one observer in mind of a battle-ship. Long a private residence, it was converted just before the war into Paris's most luxurious hotel. Some of their visitors met them in a potentially more convivial location, just around the corner, where a suite of offices had been carved out of what were normally *cabinets particuliers* above Maxim's Bar-Restaurant ('very busy every evening and night; not suitable if ladies are in the party').[11]

Venizelos had done his best to reach an understanding with the Italians; as yet he had failed. He had no personal knowledge of Wilson or his advisers, except for the inconclusive meeting with House in London in late October. When it came to the French and British Prime Ministers, Venizelos was on friendly but not quite visiting terms with them. If he needed to confer privately with Lloyd George he often thought it best to call in John Stavridi, close friend of the British Prime Minister, recently knighted and now Greek Consul-General in London once again. As for Clemenceau, it was notoriously difficult to meet the old man at all. He hoarded nearly all his astonishing energy for his public life and his Presidency of the Peace Conference. Throughout his tenure of office Clemenceau flatly refused to inhabit official residences ('I don't like living in digs,' he would explain); he lived alone in his two-floor apartment in the rue Franklin near the Palais du Trocadéro. Luckily this was not so very far from the British and the Greeks; and Venizelos had a useful route to Clemenceau by way of Apostolos Alexandris. As ambassador in Berne, Alexandris had become an intimate friend of his French opposite number, Paul Dutasta. On Clemenceau's insistence Dutasta was now Secretary-General of the Peace Conference (Conference gossip falsely alleged that he was Clemenceau's illegitimate son),[12] and the Greeks often made discreet use of their private access to the two Frenchmen at the centre of the Paris web. Although Alexandris and Stavridi were not members of the delegation, they were in Paris surprisingly often during 1919. Another mutual friend of Venizelos, Lloyd George and Clemenceau was Sir Basil Zaharoff, a Greek of Constantinople who had grown rich in the arms trade and entertained royally at his Paris house at 53, avenue Hoche, three minutes' walk from the Mercédès, five from the Majestic, and a five-minute cab ride from President Woodrow Wilson's well-guarded house, lent to him by Princess Murat, close to the Parc de Monceau.

On 16 December Venizelos had his first meeting with Wilson at the Villa Murat. He outlined the claims that Greece would put forward, then turned to an enthusiastic assessment of Wilson's League of Nations idea. Wilson encouraged him to set out the Greek claims in writing and to discuss them with Clive Day, the 'pale, slim, arid, decent'[13] economic historian who headed the Balkan experts on the American delegation. As Day's friend, Charles Seymour, wrote on 20 December, 'Clive has had a great advantage in his Balkan and Greek work from his interviews with Venizelos [who] is just as nice as he can be – priestly and paternal. I can see how he gets his reputation for great statesmanship. In this way: I think he found out very soon that Clive knew the difference between truth and fiction; realizing that his strongest asset would be *our* belief in his honesty, he determined to lay his cards on the table and speak with absolute frankness, and I think that he did. This policy was almost Bismarckian in cleverness. Any double-dealing of the kind others are trying would have been useless; now he has our sympathy. His policy is one of moderation.' Many years later Seymour added a marginal note to this letter: 'Venizelos – "Moderation"?'[14]

These were the days of President Wilson's Christmas visit to London (he was to speak at the Guildhall on 28 December) and the days when the British Foreign Office was wondering how to capitalise on Venizelos. He had made a great impression on Wilson, or so Commander Talbot reported; London should therefore consider using him as a conduit to inspire the President to see things the British way. His unusual talent for argument and persuasion, the amazing influence that he exerted on almost any interlocutor, would (so Talbot argued) have full effect on Americans who were less familiar with Europe. Talbot's suggestion reached Lord Robert Cecil, who was soon to lead the British team in the League of Nations negotiations in Paris. He agreed that London should 'work closely with Venizelos', but he had an even better idea. On Christmas Eve he argued in the Imperial War Cabinet that the League of Nations required a powerful and independent Chancellor, and that Venizelos was the man for the job. Lloyd George agreed.[15]

In 12 solid hours, on 30 December 1918, Venizelos compiled *Greece before the Peace Congress* (the definitive version in French was *La Grèce devant le Congrès de la Paix*), a text that henceforward embodied Greek claims. On Thrace he now boldly argued that at Bucharest in 1913 Greece had taken a *conciliatory attitude* towards Bulgaria and had made concessions which *might seem inexplicable*. The text was distributed to delegates at Paris in the new year but not immediately made public; rather the contrary. Kaklamanos sent personally addressed copies to British cabinet ministers and to trusted

> 'I have been assured so often that Greece wants nothing that does not belong to her that I am beginning to doubt it.'
>
> CLIVE DAY ON HIS DISCUSSIONS WITH VENIZELOS

friends. Back in Athens Venizelos's deputy, Repoulis, did not get a copy at all.

In early January British junior diplomats and American professors discussed the Greek claims among themselves. Venizelos made great use of his contacts; Clive Day (so he noted in his diary) was assured so frequently that Greece wanted 'nothing that does not belong to her' that he began to doubt it.[16] On the 8th, at lunch at the Hôtel de Crillon, Nicolson noted that the Americans favoured 'a limited concession to the Greeks in northern Epirus. Not Koritsa [Korçë] ... Some idea of giving Kavalla to the Bulgars ... Very opposed to Greece taking Western Thrace'; on 9 January, at a return meeting at the Hôtel Astoria, the Americans were 'firm on Italy surrendering Dodecanese'.[17]

Lloyd George arrived in Paris on 11 January, and things began to move. The first official meeting of the real powerhouse, the 'Council of Ten' (heads of government and foreign ministers of the United States, Britain, France, Italy and Japan) took place two days later. *The Times* published an interview with Venizelos from which Repoulis and Diomidis belatedly learned details of Greece's claims as set out in *Greece before the Peace Congress*. Meanwhile Harold Nicolson visited the Greeks at the Hôtel Mercedes, where 'T...' told him about Korçë and the ruined city of Voskopojë as centres of Greek culture in northern Epirus ('T...' might be the future President of Greece, Konstantinos Tsatsos). 'I then go in and see Venizelos. In spite of the heat in the room he wears his black silk cap ... Venizelos shows me his ethnical statistics: *It has been a point of honour with me to gather accurate statistics.*' Nicolson hinted that if Greece got Eastern and Western Thrace, the resulting frontier would be impossible to defend. *These days people don't fight geographical wars.*

Germany fought one, and you see what came of it, Venizelos replied.[18] As for Cyprus, no one mentioned it. 'We were all of us feeling our way,' wrote Lloyd George afterwards about these mid January days, 'and I had a sense that we were each of us trying to size up our colleagues, reconnoitring their respective positions, ascertaining their aims.'[19]

6

At the Conference

The Peace Conference opened on 18 January 1919, a bad day for Greece. Delegates gathered for a plenary session at the Quai d'Orsay and Venizelos was not among them. Greece, Belgium and Serbia had been furious that 'for some foolish reason'[1] Brazil, unlike all other middling Powers, was allowed three representatives. At the last moment Belgium and Serbia were allowed three as well; Greece was not. Venizelos stayed away, and had an angry meeting with Clemenceau, pointedly reminding him of the Greek troops who had just reached Ukraine in support of the French expedition.

To make matters worse, next day Venizelos had the unwelcome news from Kaklamanos that his unguarded remark in Rome had been turned against him. The Italian embassy in London was now arguing against any cession of Cyprus by Britain, just so that Italy would not have to give up the Dodecanese. Sonnino, now in Paris, reverted to the issues he had refused to discuss in Rome. In a private meeting he suggested a trade-off to Venizelos: the Italians to have what they wanted in Albania (including northern Epirus, currently claimed by Greece); Greece to have the Dodecanese and

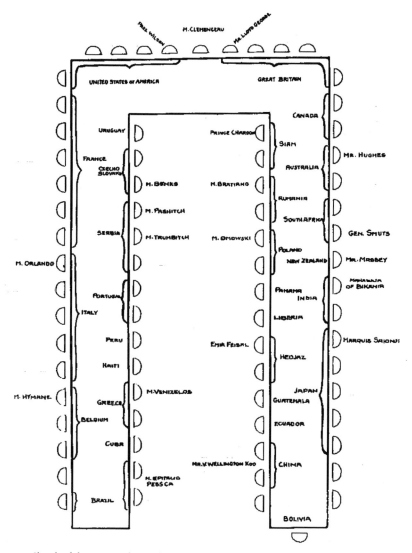

Sketch of the seating plan at the Paris Peace Conference.

Italian support for her claim to Smyrna. Had he trusted the Italians, Venizelos might have agreed, but he now knew he had no reason to trust them. He stalled, and asked Talbot and Nicolson what the British thought. Their analysis was this: Sonnino must know President Wilson favoured the Greek claim to the Dodecanese and Smyrna; fearing failure there, Sonnino evidently wanted a free run for the Italian claim in Albania, but the bargain he offered was worthless. Venizelos accepted this analysis and gave Sonnino nothing. The negotiations stalled.

Meanwhile the American experts had completed their report on Greek claims. They assumed that the Dodecanese would become Greek; also that the 1915 Treaty of London was no longer relevant, since its signatories had accepted Wilson's Four Principles and Fourteen Points as the basis for peace negotiations. The Americans dropped their earlier view that Greece should give up Kavala to Bulgaria, and accepted that at least the Korçë district of Albania should go to Greece. They were in favour of an international state of Constantinople and the Dardanelles. Thrace, however, should be Bulgarian; and there was no good reason, commercial, strategic or political, for Greece to annex Smyrna. The British had not seen this report, but they had conferred with its authors, and their advice to Venizelos was well-informed. He would have gained nothing by agreeing to support the Italian claim in Albania. Much more important was to keep on close terms with the American professors and, if possible, to dissuade them from favouring Bulgaria. Nicolson invited Venizelos to lunch with Day. Also present were two other American experts; Venizelos had 'a fierce argument' with Albert Lybyer, a young Bulgarophile who had been 'silent, somewhat remote' and longing to assert himself (two of his teachers were in the delegation). No harm was done. Venizelos was 'moderate, charming, gentle, apt. A most successful luncheon'.[2]

His initial anger over Greek representation at plenary sessions died away. Things looked different once he had been invited by Lord Robert Cecil to consider the post of Chancellor of the League of Nations (though he turned it down: Greece needed him). After that, when he talked over the representation issue with British delegates, they persuaded him to let the issue pass – but there seemed no harm in mentioning Cyprus. Venizelos neatly (and truthfully) ascribed to Sonnino the idea that the island should be given to Greece: he himself, he added, merely *hoped the moment might arrive when the British might make a beau geste by offering it*.[3] The second plenary session of the Conference was held on 25 January; Venizelos and Politis represented Greece. Committees were set up, and Greece emerged well represented, Politis, Michalakopoulos and Koromilas each finding a place.

Venizelos was soon to present Greece's case to the Council of Ten. The Americans had prepared their position; the British were now to do the same, and their position paper (written by Nicolson) favoured Greek claims in all four regions, northern Epirus, Thrace, Asia Minor (a more limited zone than that claimed by Venizelos) and the Dodecanese.[4] British military experts, on the other hand, opposed the Greek claims both in Thrace and Asia Minor. The British delegation argued it out at an internal conference at the Hôtel Astoria, concluding that if any European state was to annex Smyrna it had much better be Greece than Italy.[5]

On 3 February, with Politis at his side, Venizelos appeared before the Council of Ten. The meetings were held in Pichon's room at the Quai d'Orsay, shadowed by a brooding portrait of Maria de' Medici, lightened by a view over an inner, private garden. Venizelos had prepared himself tirelessly, working 15 or 16 hours a day. In total he spoke for nearly four hours, and the sly pleasure that he took in shaping an argument to his audience was evident once more. *La Grèce devant le Congrès de la Paix* was his text; he inserted, on this one occasion, a claim to Cyprus. But it was necessary to begin with northern Epirus, where his problem was that Greece claimed a region whose majority language – it could not be denied – was Albanian. Venizelos handed round photographs of the sponge fisheries in the Dodecanese. 'He talks gaily and simply,' Nicolson noted in his diary, 'and they look at his photograph albums which put them in a good temper.' Meanwhile he was arguing that national consciousness, not language, was the best test of ethnicity. '*Many prominent Greeks, such as Admiral Koundouriotis or my colleagues MM. Danglis and Repoulis, speak Albanian in their homes, even as Mr Lloyd George would speak Welsh to his own children*. Ll. G. beams at this. *The better test*, continues Venizelos, *is that of school attendance ... the Greek schools have a far higher ratio of attendance. And this is not in the least because the Greek schools give a better education than the Albanian schools. Not in the least. For the Albanian schools in the main centres have the benefit of American teachers!* Wilson beams delight.'[6]

On the second day Venizelos moved on to Asia Minor and began by citing Point Twelve of the Fourteen. Western Asia Minor, as claimed by Greece, contained a Greek majority which was entitled to self-determination – including the right to declare union with Greece. Overall he was not so logical and effective as he had been on the previous day, or so Nicolson thought. Other observers (there were as many as 20 in attendance) noticed that France and Britain gave Venizelos a smooth ride; he had been careful not to give offence by insisting on the issue of Cyprus. Italy, though polite, opposed him at every point. The United States firmly opposed his claims in Asia Minor. Venizelos's assessment (in a dispatch to Repoulis, written the same evening) was over-optimistic: *What I regard as certain is that we shall get Smyrna and Ayvali (with what hinterland I am not yet sure), also Cyprus and the Dodecanese ... and half of northern Epirus.*[7]

President Wilson now left for the United States, where he was to adjourn Congress. Meanwhile the Council had set up a Greek Committee to consider Venizelos's claims. Jules Cambon, its French chairman, and Nicolson, its 'technical delegate', tended to be sympathetic to Greece. It focused in turn on northern Epirus, Thrace, and Asia Minor, where the British and French favoured allocating a limited area around Smyrna to Greece; the Americans were against.[8] On 24 February Venizelos was invited to give evidence to the Committee at the Quai d'Orsay. His friendship with Nicolson and others now stood him in good stead: the Committee's minutes were private but he knew what it had been talking about. His audience – diplomats and professors alike – clustered at one end of a long table in the vast Grande Salle à Manger whose red-curtained windows looked north-west across the Seine to the Place de la Concorde and its Egyptian obelisk. Venizelos was 'overwhelmingly frank, genial and subtle. His charm lights up the room,' Nicolson wrote in his diary, 'but no real ice has been cut.' Still, the Americans were now moving towards the British and French position that both western and eastern Thrace should become Greek. After the meeting Day and Nicolson walked together across the Pont de la Concorde and so back to the Hôtel de Crillon where they studied possible Thracian frontiers. 'Somewhere,' Nicolson reflected in frustration, 'there must be a definite human desire behind all these lies and lies'; yet he never wavered in his sympathy for the Greek Prime Minister. When Venizelos had completed his evidence Nicolson and a colleague invited him and his friend Tache Ionescu to dinner at the Majestic; they 'told Balkan stories'.[9] Late in the evening they went on to a party at the dandy Boni de Castellane's pied-à-terre (at 71, rue de Lille, just round the corner from the Quai d'Orsay) 'where Bishops and statesmen, generals and philosophers, assembled in a sixteenth century atmosphere to listen to seventeenth century music struggling against twentieth century conversation.' They did not go alone. Rumours were rife that Greek anarchists wanted to assassinate Venizelos; police motor cycles followed them all the way.[10]

A few days later Nicolson and Venizelos lunched alone: 'He is distressed at the American opposition to his Smyrna claims.' Nicolson confirmed Venizelos's instinct that he must tackle President Wilson personally about Smyrna as soon as he returned to Paris.[11] Then, at the Greek Committee meeting on 11 March, Clive Day called into question the almost-agreed position on eastern and western Thrace with the new argument that frontiers in the whole region should remain undecided until a decision was reached on Constantinople (which seemed likely to be governed by the Americans themselves). This sudden American shift was immediately supported, for their own tactical reasons, by the Italians.[12]

The President was back on 14 March, now living, less grandiosely, in the rue Nitot opposite Lloyd George. Two days later Venizelos read to Nicolson the letter he was about to send to Wilson about Asia Minor, admirably written and appositely quoting the President's own speeches.[13] This letter appeared to have an astonishingly rapid effect. The American experts now found themselves pressed by their chief Samuel Mezes (but the pressure, so they understood, really came from 'higher-ups', that is, from Wilson personally) to achieve agreement over Asia Minor. At the same moment Nicolson was pressed by Hardinge, his superior in the Foreign Office, to reach an understanding with Mezes. Soon Venizelos was being assured by Colonel House in person that the United States would accept the British line in Asia Minor. Full agreement between the delegations was indeed reached on 28 March at the Hôtel de Crillon.

Venizelos did not immediately suspect any link between the new and welcome American flexibility on Asia Minor and the new firmness on Thrace, which only became evident to him more gradually. Nicolson and his colleagues on the Greek Committee observed both changes at first hand, and Clive Day privately tried to explain to Nicolson 'why it is that his delegation do not stay put'. Nicolson could not follow the explanation. Perhaps Wilson had been weighing in his own mind the Greek demands in Thrace and Asia Minor, and decided to allow the Bulgarians' ethnic claims more weight than those of the Turks. More probably, dissatisfied as he was at some decisions taken in his absence – decisions that had nothing to do with Greece – he now chose to assert his authority on two matters that affected Greece powerfully. 'Wilson insists on re-opening questions that have been settled,' Frances Stevenson (Lloyd George's mistress) noted in her diary.[14]

The Greek Committee's report was about to go to the Council of Ten, and the propaganda effort outside the boundaries of the Peace Conference built to a climax. In Constantinople in late January a seven-member Anatolian Committee had been set up, representing Greeks living outside the areas claimed by Greece, and Venizelos wrote detailed instructions on the line they were to follow.[15] Now, in late March, a persuasive little book appeared, *Greece Before the Conference, by Polybius* 'with an ethnographic map'; this was the same map drawn by Stanford's that had appeared in *Sphere* and elsewhere, reprinted in different colours to de-link it from earlier propaganda. The pseudonym 'Polybius' was meant to obscure the fact that the author was a Greek, Dimitrios Kalopothakis. Highly educated, crippled by cerebral palsy, he worked as a journalist on the *Morning Post*. Kaklamanos saw that he was wasted in London. For this text Kalopothakis earned £360 and an invitation to Paris, where he made such an impression on Venizelos and Politis that he was sent straight to Athens, there becoming director of the press office.[16]

A well-written letter in *The Times* by Ronald Burrows supporting the Greek claim to Smyrna ('we earnestly hope that the American representatives will withdraw their opposition to the English and French proposals. It lies with America to decide whether two million Christians shall be condemned to perpetual bondage') was carefully timed to precede the Greek Committee's report. All was going well, and at breakfast with the journalist Theodoros Petrakopoulos Venizelos was open enough to admit that the arrests and shootings needed to enforce mobilisation in 1917–18 had turned people against him at home. *I hope even this will be reversed by the successes and territorial gains Greece is going to obtain at the Peace Conference ... We will get Thrace; we will share the sovereignty of Constantinople with the Great Powers; we will be in Asia Minor ... Or maybe you don't want Asia Minor?* Petrakopoulos answered that most Greeks thought of Thrace as their own backyard but saw Asia Minor as a dangerous adventure. *Not all Greeks,* said Venizelos, *only some of you stiff-necked ones.*[17]

The Burrows letter produced an unwelcome response. *The Times* published a long letter by 'Smyrna Resident' denying that a Greek Mandate over Turkish territory would work; the only effective Mandatories would be Britain, France or the United States. Immediate response was called for. Using the British diplomatic bag Venizelos and Politis sent Burrows facts and figures to use in his reply. Burrows submitted his draft for Venizelos's comments by way of Gerald Talbot, who travelled to Paris with the text. Venizelos telegraphed his approval and the letter appeared on 2 April, cleverly using economic and social changes in Thessaly as evidence that Greece was capable of developing Asia Minor. The epistolary controversy ran on until it was eventually overtaken by news of the Greek occupation of Smyrna.[18]

At this crucial moment the Council of Ten ceased to function. Enraged by persistent leaks to the press, Lloyd George insisted that the Supreme Council of the Conference should henceforth consist of the four heads of government alone. They met at Wilson's house in the rue Nitot, and Clemenceau's interpreter, Paul Mantoux, kept a record. The Foreign Ministers and their various advisers continued to meet at the Quai d'Orsay as before; they were not always informed of the conversations of the Council of Four. It was to this new Council, undiluted by experts, that the Greek Committee's report was presented on 30 March. On Asia Minor there was a basis for agreement; on Thrace the report merely stated the now-irreconcilable positions of the British and French (who favoured the Greek claim) and the Americans and Italians (who opposed it).

Throughout April those concerned with western and eastern Thrace still expected that Greece would get a large part of both regions; the eventual eastern frontier would depend on decisions about Constantinople. This was the best information available to the French General Franchet d'Esperey, in Constantinople, and to General Paraskevopoulos, in Salonica, who had to try to ensure security in Thrace. In May, however, the future became more cloudy: American delegates, with continued Italian support, now insisted that no decision on any part of Thrace should be taken until Constantinople was settled. Responding to Greek worries, Clemenceau reassured Athos Romanos that he would support the Greek claim to Thrace *jusqu'au bout*, 'all the way'.[19] But what could Clemenceau do? Venizelos's nightmare was of going home with nothing at all, to see his government collapse amid the jibes of Royalist opponents.

The Americans were not alone in changing their minds. No sooner had the report reached the Council of Four than Nicolson began to reconsider Asia Minor. If Greece did not get Smyrna Venizelos would fall from power, but perhaps this had to be faced. The Greek army alone could not conquer Asia Minor; Britain could not go to its aid. He was unwittingly agreeing with Lord Curzon, who already on 25 March had written privately to Balfour: 'I cannot help thinking that this great pack of cards which is being reared [in Asia Minor] will, almost at the first blow, tumble in fragments to the ground.'[20] But Lloyd George, Clemenceau and Wilson were not interested. They had become more and more exasperated with Italian tactics. In Paris the Italians opposed and obstructed; in difficult territories – in Albania and Asia Minor, for example – Italy fomented disputes. The Dalmatian port of Fiume (Rijeka) brought matters suddenly to a head; unable after weeks of argument to persuade the Council that Italy should annex the town, on 24 April Orlando tearfully departed for Rome.

Aware of increasing favour for the Greek claim to Smyrna, Italy had been landing troops at various points on the Asia Minor coast and saying nothing about it. For the last month Venizelos had persistently warned the British and Americans that Italian intrigue was encouraging Turkish attacks on Greek communities in and around Smyrna. It now became known in Paris that two Italian warships were making for Smyrna, the city at the centre of the Greek claim. 'The Italians, by trying to steal a march ... have helped the Greeks more than they know,' Nicolson wrote on 2 May.[21]

That evening he dined with Venizelos, who talked about Athens. The political honesty that he had tried to foster had, he said, suffered a setback during the last months; he would need to clean the Augean stables on his return, to punish supporters as well as opponents. He would need a free hand. He would resign his party leadership and go to the country. A dictatorship? Nicolson mused. *Une dictature élective*, an elected dictatorship, Venizelos chuckled. *I am not a vain man, you know, but I am in a unique position. No politician has the prestige that I have.*[22]

With the sudden absence of Orlando the Council (now of Three) was free to air its Italian frustrations. Italy's secrecy encouraged rumours of Italian military movements; Venizelos's warnings ensured that they were discussed daily. The Three longed to teach the Italians a lesson. When they met on 5 May they had just received a letter from Skevos Zervos of the Delegation of the Dodecanese reporting that on Easter Sunday Italian carabinieri had broken up co-ordinated demonstrations in favour of union with Greece, and that at Rhodes the vicar-general had been killed in his church. Lloyd George said: 'We must let the Greeks occupy Smyrna. There are massacres under way and no one to protect the Greek population.' 'Do you realize,' Clemenceau interrupted, 'that Italy now has seven ships off Smyrna?' 'We had better decide this among ourselves before the Italians come back,' Lloyd George continued, 'otherwise I'm convinced they'll beat us to it.' 'I'm with you,' Clemenceau agreed. 'They must find our decisions already taken.'[23]

Next morning Lloyd George raised the issue again: 'I think we must tell M. Venizelos to send troops to Smyrna.' Wilson asked: 'Why not get them to disembark at once? Have you any objection?' 'None.' 'Nor have I,' said Clemenceau; 'should we tell the Italians?' 'I think not,' said Lloyd George.[24] Instead, Clemenceau sent a three-word telegram to Sir Basil Zaharoff: 'Vous avez Smyrne.'[25] A couple of hours later Venizelos was lying on his bed at the Hôtel Mercédès, exhausted; Nikolaos Politis, as often, was sitting beside him. Venizelos was called to the telephone; Politis took it instead. The call was from Zaharoff. 'Tell Venizelos to get ships and men ready for a landing at Smyrna. I've succeeded in getting the Supreme Council to make the decision; they'll announce it to you tomorrow. I'm telling you now so that you lose no time.'[26] Not convinced, Venizelos and Politis dressed for the Plenary Session of the Peace Conference scheduled for 3 p.m. at the Quai d'Orsay.

Lloyd George had telephoned too, urging them to arrive

The notorious and enigmatic arms dealer Sir Basil Zaharoff (1849–1936) was a friend of politicians in Britain, France and Greece. If he really promised to urge on Clemenceau the case for a Greek occupation of Smyrna, he evidently kept his word. He had his reasons. Greeks and Turks armed enthusiastically for the coming struggle, and Zaharoff sold weapons to both sides. They bought on borrowed money, however, and he was rumoured to have lost heavily in the Asia Minor catastrophe.

He was the model for Basil Bazarov in Hergé's Tintin story *The Broken Ear* (1937) and for Sir Marcus Davis in Graham Greene's *A Gun for Sale* (1936).

a little early. He was there to meet them, and asked without preamble: 'Do you have troops available?' *We have*, said Venizelos unhesitatingly; *for what purpose?* 'President Wilson, M. Clemenceau and I decided today that you are to occupy Smyrna.' *We are ready*, said Venizelos.[27] They went in to the dining room, where the Session was about to begin. Lloyd George beckoned to General Sir Henry Wilson, Chief of the Imperial General Staff, and told him what was agreed. 'I asked Lloyd George if he realised that this was starting another war,' General Wilson noted in his diary. After the Plenary Session he took Venizelos to his office at the Astoria to decide details of the operation. 'I insisted on the fact that it was a Greek affair, under Greek command, and that there was danger of opposition both from the Italians and the Turks, and that both Governments ought to be warned ... Of course the whole thing is *mad*,' he concluded. That evening Venizelos sent off three cipher telegrams, including one to Repoulis and one to Paraskevopoulos at Salonica.[28]

At 11 a.m. on 7 May General Wilson, expecting to meet the Three and Venizelos for a final meeting on Smyrna, laughed to see that Orlando was entering President Wilson's study just ahead of him, ready to turn the Three back into Four. Lloyd George emerged hastily and told the General to divert Venizelos to his own house across the road. After an uncomfortable half-hour the meeting of the Four was adjourned, Orlando departed, and the Three crossed the road to meet Venizelos. Clemenceau told him formally: 'We intend Greek troops to be landed at Smyrna to prevent massacres and forestall an Italian landing.' There was a division in Macedonia, Venizelos said, ready to move because it was about to be sent to Ukraine. Lloyd George wanted to know if that was all he had. Greece could spare two divisions, Venizelos answered, but, if afterwards asked to intervene in Thrace, would then have to withdraw troops from the Ukraine. 'There's no question of going into Thrace,' said Clemenceau sharply, 'we don't want that. It would start a fight with the Bulgarians ...' Venizelos then said: *It's important to manage it so that the Turks are not warned till the last minute. I know these Turkish officers: if they don't get orders to resist, they won't. As for the people of Smyrna, their attitude will be very friendly.* 'Isn't it better to warn the Turks?' said Clemenceau. 'It's more proper,' President Wilson admitted, 'but it also makes the landing riskier.' Lloyd George now turned to Venizelos. 'Can you make your preparations secretly?' *Certainly we can. When we were asked to send troops to Odessa, we got together enough tonnage to transport ten thousand men. Tightly packed, I admit: the Greek soldier isn't too demanding in that way.* Clemenceau wanted clarity: 'We're saying nothing to the Italians for the moment?' 'It's important to keep this whole business as secret as possible,' Wilson insisted.[29]

Nicolson heard of the Smyrna decision the same afternoon: 'a personal triumph for Venizelos' was his summary.[30] At the same moment, Kaklamanos was in London with Lord Curzon at the Foreign Office, raising the issue of the anti-Greek propaganda that filled the Italian newspapers. A secretary entered with a message which Curzon paused to read. 'I'll tell you what I have just learned,' said Curzon, 'because this will be the best possible cure for the irritation we are discussing. The Council of Four has decided to authorise Greece to land troops at Smyrna.' Kaklamanos telegraphed his congratulations to Paris, and received the following reply: *Strictly confidential: ambassador to decipher. Imperative keep Curzon information absolutely secret. Authorisation granted Three, not Four. Venizelos.*[31]

It was a busy day in Paris. The excuse for the rapid adjournment of the 11 a.m. meeting had been (as Maurice Hankey put it in Civil Service prose) 'for the purpose of proceeding to Versailles for the presentation of the Treaty to the Germans', an uncomfortable rendezvous for both sides.[32] That same evening, when all was over, Venizelos managed to have a private talk with Clemenceau, saying that he hoped President Wilson would continue to insist on the transfer of the Dodecanese to Greece; *I spoke of Wilson,* Venizelos noted, *because I quite understood that France and England were in a weak position on this issue owing to the Treaty of London. Clemenceau interrupted me. He too, he told me emphatically, was determined to insist that Italy must not keep the Dodecanese.*[33]

As for Lloyd George, he invited Venizelos to dinner on 9 May and exhorted him: 'There are great possibilities for Greece in the Near East and so far as possible you need to be stronger militarily to be able to take advantage of them. We want the mandate for Constantinople to be taken by America, which will not at all prevent the transfer of Constantinople to Greek sovereignty at some later appropriate date.' *I told him,* Venizelos noted, *that if they would provide the financial means we could not only increase the Greek army to 15 divisions ... but also, once we have Smyrna and Thrace and other new territories, we could assemble at least another five new divisions.*[34]

'I resolved to write these things down, as of vital importance to the nation's future, and if possible to continue this diary until the end of the crisis. A good resolution ... but can I keep it?'
VENIZELOS'S MAY 1919 DIARY

The Three became Four again when Orlando reappeared at the morning meeting on 10 May. He was asked to agree that all Allied troops should leave Corfu (Venizelos had suggested to Clemenceau that this would be the only way to get the Italians off the island). No one mentioned Smyrna. There were meetings on Saturday afternoon and Sunday from which, somehow, Orlando was absent. Venizelos was present at both, and a few final arrangements were made.

On the 11th Balfour stood in for Lloyd George, who was spending the day with Frances Stevenson at Fontainebleau. Clemenceau, who had more sympathy for the Italian Premier than his Anglo-Saxon colleagues (and had privately told Venizelos that he was seriously worried about the Italian reaction) now argued irritably that they must delay the landing till Orlando had been told. The others hesitated, until Wilson said finally: 'We must tell the Italians tomorrow.' Balfour, taking advantage of the fact that he did not see minutes of these meetings, asked innocently: 'What was the origin of our decision? Did the Greeks initially mention their fear of massacres in Asia Minor?' *No*, said Venizelos, *I was consulted when the discussion was already under way.* 'Aren't you afraid that your landing at Smyrna will set off massacres elsewhere in the country?' *No*, said Venizelos again, his tone perhaps defensive, *the Turks respect force.* Balfour said coolly: 'I don't mean to go over the decision again; the question is how to put it into effect.'[35]

The next meeting of the Four was at 11 a.m. on the 12th; Lloyd George reappeared only ten minutes beforehand. *I had just enough time to tell him my thoughts on what was going on*, Venizelos recorded. *I asked him particularly to guard against the Greek expedition becoming an Allied one. He assured me, unhesitatingly, that the agreement of St Jean de Maurienne was not really binding … I came away full of optimism.*[36] At this meeting the Three at last admitted to Orlando that the Smyrna landing had been ordered and cajoled him into agreeing that no British, French or Italian troops need join it. There was no more talk of delay.[37]

That afternoon Paraskevopoulos telegraphed to confirm that the first division was ready to leave Salonica next morning. Venizelos had fully achieved his aim: he had approval for the Greek occupation of Smyrna, an occupation that might in due time become an annexation. 'Venizelos is using the three Frocks for his own ends,' Henry Wilson commented:[38] the three Frocks (Lloyd George, Clemenceau and President Wilson) knew it and were willing to be used. Clemenceau wrote of 'Venizelos, child of Ulysses and Calypso and duly permeated with Hellenic guile.'[39]

That evening Venizelos, bursting with happiness, was seen in the corridors of the Mercédès hugging Spyros Spyromilios, an old comrade-in-arms from Salonica who was now a member of the Northern Epirus delegation. He found time for a quiet talk with Christos Kesaris, correspondent of the Athens daily *Estia*. *We were on the edge of the abyss,* said Venizelos, *and we have been saved. Now we are among the great.* 'The dream of Pericles, the union of Hellenism, is becoming a reality,' Kesaris replied. 'We owe it to you, Prime Minister.' *Yes, yes, but I could have done nothing without the Greek people – excellent, admirable people! If only their politicians prove worthy of them.* Those who visited Venizelos that day, said Kesaris, carried away an unforgettable impression of overflowing joy.[40]

On 14 May Kaklamanos in London was authorised by Venizelos to break the secrecy surrounding the impending landing: *Please give Lady Crosfield my congratulations on the liberation of her homeland and my thanks to Sir Arthur for all that we owe him.* Sir Arthur replied at once, promising to give the news at dinner to 'Mrs Schilizzi and Miss Schilizzi'. Zaharoff, now in London, was informed as well. He thanked Kaklamanos jovially and added: 'I believe, in all modesty, that this resulted from my initiative. I have telegraphed my heart-felt thanks to Clemenceau and Lloyd George.'[41] The news broke in Athens on the same day. On the 16th the Paris and London newspapers were full of it, and Nicolson reported renewed jubilation at the Mercédès. Next day there was another party at Boni de Castellane's, at which the diplomat-poet Paul Claudel was present and his poetry was read. After-wards Venizelos 'looking ill and tired, but happy' shared a cab with Nicolson, and said: *Greece can only find her real future from the moment when she is astride the Aegean.*[42]

During these hectic weeks he had somehow found time to notice a preliminary meeting at the Académie des Inscrip-tions et Belles-Lettres whose purpose was to set up a world association of national academies. Greece had none, and Venizelos sent off a hasty telegram to his Education Minister: *Start Academy quickly.*[43]

And now, having disposed of Smyrna for the present, the Three took part in a day-long series of meetings on both sides of the rue Nitot to sketch the frontiers of Armenia and divide up the rest of Asia Minor, in a scene memorably character-ised by Balfour, who was not invited, as 'three ignorant men with a child to lead them'. Nicolson (the 'child') was present because his maps and geographical knowledge were wanted. At these meetings Lloyd George was still asserting his inten-tion 'to give Greece the island of Cyprus'. French approval would be needed, Clemenceau teased. 'If you can make this gift to Greece,' Wilson added, 'it will be a great thing.'[44] But a storm now broke on Lloyd George, who in his dealings on Asia Minor and Cyprus was going far beyond what his colleagues would accept. British and Indian Empire delegates threatened resignation. The Council of Four was told firmly of the feeling among Muslims, exacerbated by the Greek landing at Smyrna, that the Peace Conference was taking sides against Islam. Britain dared not forget that its Indian Empire made it the world's largest Muslim power, nor that Indian troops had played a large part in its war effort.[45] Muslims were not alone in objecting to the decisions recently taken. Most of the British Cabinet travelled to Paris for a heated argument on 19 May. Lloyd George capitulated, and announced to the Council of Four the Cabinet's formal decision that the British government would not support the partition of Turkey.

Venizelos had sent off a proclamation to the Greeks of Smyrna, begging them to show moderation to their Turkish neighbours. In the event the Greek landing was far from peaceful. There were lootings and killings by Greek troops; there were many civilian atrocities. When he and Politis dined with Nicolson and Lloyd George's private secretary Philip Kerr, Venizelos admitted to receiving reports of 'lack of discipline' among Greek troops: 'They seem to have behaved pretty badly,' Nicolson comments, 'and there are rumours of civilians having been killed … He is anxious and depressed.'[46] Venizelos knew that the truth was even more serious than this (Repoulis, acting Prime Minister, was already in Smyrna, sent there by Venizelos to sort things out) but he continued to deny it. As late as 29 May he wrote to Clemenceau (as President of the Conference) rejecting the atrocity reports. Forwarded by Politis to Kaklamanos, this letter appeared in the *Daily Telegraph*, *Manchester Guardian* and *Morning Post*.

The newspapers' own correspondents were better informed, as Venizelos was soon forced to admit. Because the facts emerged slowly, against a background of denials by himself and others, the controversy mounted. A sign of his loss of stature was the arrival in Paris towards the end of June of John Stavridi, evidently needed to rebuild the broken intimacy with Lloyd George. Ronald Burrows, one of Greece's most assiduous propagandists, now wrote from London urging Venizelos that he must take some new initiative. Accordingly he instructed Kaklamanos to propose to the Foreign Office a bilateral inquiry into the atrocities and to prepare Burrows for the results: *I hope it will show, in spite of bad behaviour caused by memories of ancestral enmity, that our army's attitude has in general been much better than suggested by the incidents of the first few days. If it proves that these incidents were worse than I thought, I would urge, above all else, severe punishment for the guilty as the only means of restoring our damaged prestige.*[47] The Foreign Office would not play this game, however. Instead the Four Powers set up a joint inquiry.

The Italian government had fallen, and Orlando's successor designated the new Foreign Minister, Tommaso Tittoni, as delegation leader in Paris. The Three assumed there would be no change in the Italians' general attitude, and President Wilson drafted an ultimatum to greet him: the Italians must decide now whether they were with the Allies or not; if they were, they must withdraw their troops from Asia Minor and 'we can in no case entertain their claim to the Dodecanesos'.[48] But Tittoni and his government wanted to solve foreign problems, not create them; and unlike his predecessors he could work with Venizelos. On 29 July (Wilson having meanwhile left Paris for the last time) Venizelos and Tittoni reached an agreement on mutual support at Paris for the aims of Italy and Greece. Greece would back Italian claims to a mandate over Albania and to terrritory in south-western Asia Minor;

Italy would cede the Dodecanese except Rhodes and would support the Greek claim to northern Epirus and to Thrace as well as the occupation of western Asia Minor up to an agreed border.[49]

Ever since March the Americans had blocked agreement on Thrace, and on 19 July the Central Committee (set up to complete the work of the Greek Committee and others) had reported an irresoluble two-two split. Italy and the United States wanted Bulgaria to retain western Thrace; Britain and France wanted the territory to go to Greece. Balfour wrote to House in an attempt to solve the impasse; Venizelos himself wrote to Wilson in Washington, commenting in a letter to Repoulis soon afterwards, *He is a very stubborn man.*[50]

Then came the pact with Tittoni. On 31 July, at the Council of Ten which had once more replaced the secretive Four, Tittoni duly supported the Greek position on Thrace. Frank L Polk, the new head of the American delegation, found himself isolated. Polk attributed the Tittoni-Venizelos pact to British scheming; Wilson, from across the Atlantic, was to describe it as 'little less than intolerable'.[52]

'Venizelos realizes the difficulty of the future but must go back from the Conference "with the bacon" in order to hold his position in Greece – where he has martial law and his monarchist enemies locked up.'
CHARLES SEYMOUR ON 2 JULY 1919[51]

Tittoni happened to suggest variations on ethnic grounds to the proposed borders of eastern Thrace. The resulting discussions produced a new frontier between Bulgaria and Thrace on which, refreshingly, all delegations agreed. As to the fate of Thrace itself, Polk and Venizelos reached an understanding. Greece would have eastern Thrace, or most of it;

western Thrace should either be an international state, or (if Venizelos could persuade Wilson to prefer this solution) it should be Greek, Bulgaria being guaranteed right of access to Aegean ports. Wilson by telegram rejected both solutions, and made a counter-proposal which, on 1 September at the Supreme Council, Clemenceau in turn rejected. He had promised to support Greece 'all the way', and he kept his promise. This final stalemate was neatly resolved by Balfour. 'I don't get sufficiently excited by these meetings,' Balfour once complained;[53] he could see further beyond them than most and perhaps saw a world without Wilson. He proposed that since everyone now agreed on its borders, Thrace should be temporarily taken over by the Powers, who would decide its fate later. No one objected, and the treaty was presented in this form to Bulgarian delegates in Paris. Venizelos wrote once more to Wilson in a last attempt to persuade him that he was wrong on western Thrace and that the territory should go to Greece; but Wilson suffered a paralysing stroke on 2 October, and no reply came.

The Peace Conference was now running down, and in early November the office of the Greek delegation at the Hôtel Mercédès closed. The long-awaited treaty with Germany had been signed on 28 June, in an atmosphere of ceremonial tension, at the Hall of Mirrors at Versailles. Austria's treaty was signed at Saint-Germain-en-Laye in early September. More significant to Greece than either of these was the Treaty of Neuilly, by which peace with Bulgaria was formally re-established. This was signed on 27 November, and on the same day Greece and Bulgaria signed a convention on the voluntary exchange of minorities, a partial precedent for later Asia Minor arrangements. One other event of 1919 must be noted. Venizelos had recently made the acquaintance of

Emmanouil Zervoudakis, a wealthy Greek businessman who lived sometimes in London, sometimes in Nice. His daughter, Kathleen, was of just the same age as Sofoklis Venizelos. Zervoudakis and his wife Despina decided to spend February 1919 in Paris and happened to choose the Hôtel Mercédès. They met Sofoklis, liked him, and sent a photograph of him to Kathleen. Her response was not encouraging – she commented that his lips were too thick – but they invited him to stay with them at San Remo, where they were renting Lady Mexborough's Castello Devachan. He stayed three weeks, and had another holiday in Nice later in the summer. By then the couple had fallen in love.[54]

7

The Catastrophe and the Treaty of Lausanne

One of Venizelos's telegrams on the night of 6 May 1919 confirmed his choice of Aristidis Stergiadis, a fellow-lawyer from Crete, currently Governor-General of Epirus, as High Commissioner in Smyrna. It would be a hard task to represent Greek civilian government in a region held by Greek troops and theoretically administered by the Ottoman Empire. Stergiadis left Ioannina only on 17 May and travelled slowly. Nearly a week later he took over Smyrna from Repoulis, who had spent three uncomfortable days restoring order after the anarchy of the landing.

In a hortatory letter from Paris Venizelos urged colleagues to make full use in their publicity and propaganda of the classical history of Asia Minor, the conquest by Alexander, the glories of Pergamon; at the Supreme Council he appealed to the millennial tendency of Greeks to spread their culture eastwards.[1] That was history. Some elsewhere were looking to the modern state of the peninsula and its Turkish population, and were angered by talk of partition at Paris; the Greek occupation of Smyrna concentrated this anger. Mustafa Kemal (later known as Atatürk), native of Salonica, a brave soldier and a clear thinker, impatient at the impotence of the Imperial government at Constantinople, brought together delegates from the eastern vilayets at Erzurum. On 7 August they declared their intention to fight for an undivided Asia Minor.

The Allied inquiry into events surrounding the Smyrna landing confirmed much of what the newspapers had reported and Venizelos and his colleagues had repeatedly denied; it also advised ending the Greek occupation. It was not published. British and French governments ought not to have been surprised by the bitter resistance to Greek occupation – their embassies and consulates had predicted it – but they were gradually becoming rattled. They had encouraged Greece to fight the old Ottoman Empire for a settlement that they themselves were less and less inclined to insist on. The French, more quickly than the British, foresaw the need for good relations with the new Turkey. The Allies salved their consciences by imposing tight limits on what the Greek army could do, even when responding to attack.

> 'I told him straight out that he had ruined his country and himself by going to Smyrna, and the poor man agreed.'
>
> SIR HENRY WILSON ON VENIZELOS

Venizelos spent much of October in London on what was said to be a private visit, one that entailed frequent meetings with Lloyd George and others. The month ended with a gloomy conversation with General Sir Henry Wilson, who 'told him straight out that he had ruined his country and himself by going to Smyrna'. Venizelos blamed his difficulties on the new French desire to befriend Turkey; Wilson was not persuaded.[2]

In general Venizelos remained optimistic. As 1919 turned into 1920 he was reasonably confident of northern Epirus and the Dodecanese. He had not secured Thrace, however; the Greek army was heavily committed there (and in Asia Minor), draining men and money needed by the struggling economy. He had not lost his faith in propaganda: in autumn 1919 he had urged Kaklamanos to publish a booklet in two languages, *The Question of Thrace* and *La question de Thrace*, and it appeared while Thrace was in limbo. Early in 1920 Venizelos met Victor Seligman, an enterprising Oxford undergraduate who was earning his fees by writing pro-Greek propaganda. Seligman's book *The Victory of Venizelos* was published on 24 May to ecstatic reviews, one of which was entitled 'Eleutherios the Liberator', and another 'The King who Betrayed his Country'.[3] But in Greece martial law and censorship were still in force. Demobilisation, for which so many young men longed, was a mirage. And Venizelos himself could not go home for long. He was trapped by barren diplomacy, by the endless little conferences following the big Conference that shifted interminably from one Western-European city to another. He had little time for Greek politics, whether the administrative failings of local and national government or the private life of King Alexander, who, against the government's forceful advice, had secretly married Aspasia Manou. This love match was the first marriage of Greek royalty with a

Alexander, the King chosen by Venizelos, is famous only for his love affair with Aspasia Manou and his tragic death. Aspasia was the niece of Venizelos's maverick supporter at Theriso, Konstantinos Manos, who fell in the Second Balkan War; what mattered more in 1919 was that her father was a Royalist colonel. Against the government's wishes the pair married on 4 November 1919; Alexander died eleven months later, leaving Aspasia pregnant. Their child Alexandra (1921–93) was to become Queen of Yugoslavia.

With his triumphal entry into Adrianople, three months before his death, Alexander came closer to Constantinople than any other reigning monarch of modern Greece.

Greek commoner, and the government's impotent opposition to it now seems like incompetence.

In mid-February 1920 Venizelos was in London for an Allied conference that attempted to decide the fate of the Ottoman Empire. Clemenceau's government had been replaced by that of Alexandre Millerand; France now stood firmly against the partition of Turkey and was therefore unsympathetic to the Greek occupation of Smyrna. It was clear, too, that whatever the government in Constantinople might do, Kemal's nationalists would forcibly oppose Allied terms that included a Greek occupation. On 19 March Winston Churchill (Lloyd George's Secretary of State for War) and General Wilson went to see Venizelos and put this to him frankly. They asked whether he could impose the projected peace terms on Turkey without British and French help, and stressed what Greece was risking with the continuing occupation of Asia Minor as well as Thrace. They made it clear, Wilson recorded, that Britain would help 'neither in men nor in money ... I told him he was going to ruin his small country'. Venizelos reassured them that the Greeks could do it. He seemed to rely less on military logic than on faith: his faith in the strength and fertility of the Greeks, which within a century would raise the population of Smyrna above that of the rest of Turkey; his faith in the mountaineers of western Greece, who had formed the backbone of the mercenary forces of the ancient Persian Empire and were now to be implanted on the wild borderland between Greeks and Turks.[4]

As Venizelos leaned on Lloyd George, the British Prime Minister leaned on Venizelos. So it was that in late April, when the peace terms to be imposed on the Ottoman Empire were finally and formally approved at the San Remo Conference (at Castello Devachan, where Sofoklis Venizelos and Kathleen

Zervoudaki had fallen in love) Lloyd George insisted, over French and Italian doubts, that the Greek army should continue in Asia Minor; it was also agreed without argument that Eastern Thrace should be awarded to Greece. Western Thrace, formerly Bulgarian, formed no part of the treaty with Turkey, but the Allies decided at the same time that it should go to Greece as well. Venizelos had the result he wanted, and wrote to his old supporter Ronald Burrows to tell him of the decision. Burrows, though dying, replied with undiminished enthusiasm: 'I see from a telegram that you are taking back the good news in triumph to Greece. That is your last battle: the recreation of a united Hellas ... Ah well! It may be that your sweet reasonableness will win them in the end.'[5]

After an all-too-brief respite in Athens Venizelos was back in London on 14 June 1920. It was an ominous day: for the first time Turkish nationalist forces attacked weakly-held British positions at the Straits. Under pressure from his own ministers Lloyd George repeated his prepared warning that the Greeks were on their own. Venizelos again asserted that Greece could manage it, and Lloyd George was 'as much convinced as ever that the Greeks are splendid soldiers and the Turks are perfectly useless. It is a most dangerous obsession,' wrote Sir Henry Wilson. But now at last Venizelos had Lloyd George and Wilson where he wanted them, in need of Greek help, and at an informal and well-fed Anglo-French conference at Lympne, on 20 June, he took them to the next step. Agreeing that Greek troops could relieve the British at the Straits by a northward attack on Bandırma, he demanded that in return the Greeks should also have a free hand to attack eastwards, across the occupation frontier, as strategy dictated. The result, he argued, would be to coerce the Turks to sign the treaty.[6] Next day the conference took the ferry to

Boulogne, became a meeting of the Supreme Council, and confirmed these decisions.[7]

Early in July there was still another conference, at Spa in Belgium, at which Venizelos pressed that one or two Greek divisions from Asia Minor should occupy eastern Thrace: they could do it in two weeks. 'He thinks that the whole country, roughly west of a line Brussa–Smyrna, ought to be handed over to the Greeks. He thinks that he will next occupy Eastern Thrace up to the Chatalja lines,' Wilson noted drily; 'then, later, he thinks he ought to have Constantinople.' But at 2.30 p.m. on 10 July, as the conference was breaking up, 'Venizelos came into my room in a state of excitement and anger, to show me a telegram he had just received ... that the Greeks, against all Venizelos's orders, had occupied Brussa. We did not want this.' [8] Wilson never realised that this was theatre: Venizelos had held back the news until his suggestion about Thrace had been accepted. Bursa [Wilson's 'Brussa'] actually fell two days earlier (Sofoklis Venizelos was there).

But the promise was kept; almost within the fortnight, King Alexander triumphantly and peacefully entered Adrianople, capital of eastern Thrace. The seaport of Dedeağaç, now the easternmost city of mainland Greece, was renamed Alexandroupolis in his honour.

On 10 August the peace treaty with the Ottoman Empire was at last signed at Sèvres. Greece formally gained eastern Thrace and all the eastern Aegean islands. Smyrna would be administered by Greece on Turkey's behalf; after five years the region might vote for full annexation to Greece. On the same day a 'little' Greco-Italian treaty was signed that would in due course transfer the Dodecanese to Greece. Venizelos could claim that his 18 months of unremitting diplomacy had borne fruit. After two nights in Paris he set out for home, on what he surely hoped would be his last international journey for a while. At the Gare de Lyon, as he was about to board his train for Italy, he was shot; one bullet lodged in his shoulder, a second in his thigh. His attackers were two Royalist army officers, dismissed, like many others, when the Venizelists triumphed in 1917.

In the Greek capital there was an immediate and violent reaction to this news from Paris. Venizelist reservists roamed the streets. Ion Dragoumis, recently returned from internment in Corsica, driving through the city late at night, was taken from his car by gendarmes and shot dead in what was universally assumed to be a reprisal for the attack on Venizelos at the Gare de Lyon. *I don't want to be avenged*,[9] Venizelos protested impotently from his hospital bed. Sofoklis rushed from Smyrna to Paris – a five-day journey – and accompanied his father back to Greece. If Dragoumis's death was investigated at all, no prosecution resulted.

Venizelos now presented the terms of the Treaty of Sèvres to the Greek Parliament and confirmed that the long-delayed elections would be held precisely two months later. Parliament pronounced him 'benefactor and saviour of Greece'. 'Greater Greece and Eleftherios Venizelos are two expressions with the same meaning,' added Themistoklis Sofoulis, President of the Chamber.[10] Thrace, it was decided, must be annexed immediately so that its Greek-speaking inhabitants could vote; unconstitutionally, and although Venizelos (in opposition in 1916) had objected to an identical manoeuvre, he now made arrangements for serving soldiers to vote.

Aspasia Manos, her marriage to King Alexander no longer secret, was with him at Tatoi near Athens and pregnant with their first child. There, at the end of September, while strolling in the gardens, the young King was bitten by a monkey. The bite became infected; in the course of October he became so ill that the government reluctantly allowed his mother to visit him. She set out from Lausanne, but he died on 25 October before she reached Athens.[11]

It was evident during the King's life that the government did not know how to deal with him. The incompetence did not end with his death. Venizelos postponed the election by a week, hastily appointed Koundouriotis (one of the Salonica triumvirate) as regent, and telegraphed to ask Alexander's younger brother, Paul, to take the throne. It was impossible for Paul to accept: his father and eldest brother had not renounced their claims. There was no time to consider further options. The monarchy, which had not openly been an election issue at all, suddenly became the only issue. Venizelos spoke of the choice between himself and the exiled Constantine, and threatened, if defeated, to retire from politics.

When at last the election was held on 14 November the result was a mirror image of the victory of 1910. The Liberals won 120 seats, their combined opponents 246. Venizelos himself lost his seat, as did many of his closest collaborators. Foreign commentators, for whom Venizelos was the hero of Greece and the victor of the Peace Conference, were stunned. A few observers had warned earlier in the year that the Liberals risked defeat; even these were surprised by the scale of it. Henry Wilson accurately called this 'a great defeat for Lloyd George, as he had put his shirt on the old Greek'.[12]

Penelope Delta, Benakis's daughter, called on Venizelos next day. In her diary she described the scene: Repoulis on the sofa, groaning, his head in his hands; Tsirimokos, a mountain of jelly, ineffectively soothing him; and Venizelos as eloquent as ever in explaining his defeat. *I really thought I had the people with me, that in the great work in progress*

EMMANOUIL AND PENELOPE BENAKIS

When Venizelos burst into Greek politics in 1910, so did Emmanouil Benakis (1843–1929), wealthy Greek-Egyptian businessman, head of the Alexandria Chamber of Commerce. Like Venizelos he asserted Greek citizenship and stood for the Assembly; from 1911 he ran the new Ministry of National Economy, and was afterwards Mayor of Athens. In 1916 he bravely stayed in Athens when Venizelos went to Salonica and was imprisoned by the Royalists as a traitor. In 1920 he shared Venizelos's exile. His house (bequeathed to Greece by his son, the art collector Antonis Benakis) is now the Benakis Museum.

Benakis's daughter Penelope Delta (1874–1941) was a children's writer; her *Trelantonis*, 'Naughty Tony', embroiders her brother's boyhood adventures. She also gathered oral history records of the wars in Macedonia, Ukraine and Asia Minor, and was a close friend of Venizelos in the 1920s and 1930s. Her notebooks are full of sidelights on current events, including the death of Ion Dragoumis in 1920 (to which her father's unguarded reaction was 'Beaten up, surely, not killed?'). She took poison on the day German troops entered Athens, 27 April 1941. Chrysanthos (1881–1949), a longstanding friend, once Metropolitan of Trebizond, officiated at her funeral.

She had met Dragoumis (a member of the Greek consular service who had secretly aided the guerillas in Macedonia), when he was serving in Alexandria in 1905. They had a brief and passionate affair. Prominent in Athens as a writer and journalist of independent and firmly anti-Venizelist opinions, he was exiled to Corsica in 1917.

Delta's daughter Virginia married Alexandros Zannas (initiator of the National Defence movement at Salonica in 1915, and Air Minister 1929–32) who shared Venizelos's final exile in 1935.

the people were behind me. I was mistaken: the people were exhausted, wounded. I don't blame them; I asked for sacrifices beyond their powers. I have been crushed. I haven't the strength to fight back any more. He had promised to leave Greece, he continued, and he would go at once, because there were serious disturbances in the streets of Athens, and the Prime Minister, old Dimitrios Rallis, had written to warn him that public order could not be ensured while he remained.[13]

The dangers were real, to judge by the fact that Venizelos

had a hundred companions in his hasty exodus on 17 November. Many left without money or baggage. Their transport was the yacht *Narcissus*, chartered by Helena Schilizzi (who had arrived in Athens on 20 April for an indefinite stay). Benakis helped with this arrangement; he and Repoulis were among the hundred who crowded into the 14 cabins of the *Narcissus*, women in the beds, men on the floor, for a three-day voyage to Messina in Sicily. The captain had not been warned where he was going or how many passengers he would have: they had hardly enough coal and very little food (which did not matter much; there were fearful storms and everyone was seasick). At Messina the party stayed over-

> 'I really thought I had the people with me. I was mistaken: the people were exhausted, wounded... . I asked for sacrifices beyond their powers.'
>
> **VENIZELOS TO PENELOPE DELTA ON HIS DEFEAT IN 1920**

night and then took a special train to Nice, where Venizelos was invited to stay with Despina Zervoudakis; others, including Helena Schilizzi, found off-season accommodation in the hotels. Sofoklis Venizelos left the group at Messina and went direct to Paris to join Kathleen Zervoudakis. They returned to Nice together and were married on 27 December.

As for Eleftherios Venizelos, not long before the election Virginia Benakis, wife of his trusted ally, had asked him why he did not marry again. *Don't ask the impossible. I have loved only one woman, the mother of my sons. I lost her,* said Venizelos. *Now I am wedded to politics. I don't want any ties. I have to be free.*[14] At the ideal moment, therefore, when he had sworn to reject politics and in any case politics had rejected him, Despina Zervoudakis gave Venizelos a piece of information of which, allegedly, he was quite unaware: Helena Schilizzi, who for seven years had supported Greek and Venizelist causes with her considerable inherited wealth, had even (in 1919) given her house in Upper Brook Street to be the new Greek embassy in London, had spent several months in his close proximity in Athens and had now paid for and shared his escape to Nice, was in love with him and wanted to marry him. She was 11 years younger than he was; he had thought her younger still.

In Athens, Rallis at once announced a referendum on the recall of King Constantine, although a joint note from the Allies threatened to interpret a positive result as approval of Constantine's 'disloyal attitude and conduct' during the war.[15] Constantine claimed 99 per cent approval and returned immediately. Allied diplomats tried, but sometimes failed, to ignore him.

The election campaign had only intermittently questioned Venizelos's Greater Greece policy. Afterwards there was no falling-off. Constantine's return was the sign for a new offensive east of Smyrna. But British and French backing for Greece, half-hearted at best, could now be explained away by these governments as a reward for Venizelos's wartime support, a response to his personal diplomacy. Accordingly, the note quoted above asserted 'complete liberty in dealing with the situation' of Constantine's return, a blunt threat to withdraw financial and moral support for the Asia Minor venture. New Franco-British talks about Turkey began in late January 1921, and Venizelos was invited to be at hand. He, Sir John Stavridi, Lloyd George and a delegation of 'unredeemed' Greeks con-cocted the idea of a separate Greek state of Thrace and Asia Minor, whose real aim (like that of the Provisional Govern-ment in Salonica) would be to drive Constantine out.[16] This was fantasy. The true questions were these: since the fading Ottoman Empire had not ratified the Treaty of Sèvres, must it be revised? And must the Allies continue a policy that, in effect, supported Greece against Turkey? The answers were becoming clearer. Staying at the Majestic, which had been the British delegation's stronghold in 1919, Venizelos had a visit from his friend Nicolson, who warned him that the Treaty *would* be revised, and then from Lloyd George's private secretary Philip Kerr, who insisted that Greece must find a frontier that she could defend alone. Next day, having talked with Lloyd George in person, Venizelos wrote privately to Rallis recommending this approach. The conference decided that there should be another conference, in London; Greece and Turkey would be invited, and the Turkish delegation must include Kemal's nationalists.

> *Question*: 'How do you explain that Venizelos was summoned to Paris to discuss the Sèvres treaty?' *W L Westermann*: 'They could not keep Venizelos away. You cannot keep that man away, where Greek interests are concerned.'
> PUBLIC LECTURE AT PHILADELPHIA ON 28 JANUARY 1921[17]

By now the dying Rallis had given way to Nikolaos Kalogeropoulos as Prime Minister. Real power lay with the War Minister, Dimitrios Gounaris, who had been interned in Corsica in 1917, escaped to Italy, and in late 1920 returned during the last stage of the election campaign, consumed with hatred of Venizelos, to resume leadership of what was now the People's Party.

The new government relieved all Venizelist senior officers of their commands, and its delegation in London refused to admit Venizelos to the next conference. He offered himself instead as a representative of the 'unredeemed' Greeks, his new separatist friends, but no invitation was forthcoming. In any case no solution emerged. The Greeks were more intransigent than the Turks, and soon broke off negotiations by ordering a general advance eastwards into the Turkish heartlands.

Gounaris became Prime Minister on 8 April. Anti-Venizelist army officers were given extra seniority, and memorials were planned for those executed under Venizelos's rule. Meanwhile Mustafa Kemal was growing in military strength; newly backed by Soviet friendship he turned his full attention on the Greeks whose weary army, now deprived of many experienced officers, showed signs of desperation. At a new meeting in London in early June a side-effect of these changes became evident. Britain, still committed at the Straits, wanted to save her own position by making friends with Turkey as Italy and France had already done. Venizelos again advised behind the scenes, and his hearers' conclusions were that Greece could hold on in Asia Minor for six months at the most. London offered mediation on terms that would include Greek withdrawal from Asia Minor and retention of Thrace, and Venizelos wrote to Athens to urge acceptance.

Gounaris politely refused, and authorised a new offensive whose desperate aim was to smash the Turkish nationalists for good. Greek troops bravely advanced almost within reach of Ankara before being driven back to Afyonkarahisar, where, astonishingly, they were to hold out for nearly a year.

Helena Schilizzi, many years afterwards, remembered a dinner given by the Greek community in London, in December 1912, at which she was first introduced to Venizelos. On that occasion 'we talked about the aubergines.'[18] They married in London on 15 September 1921. He had received death threats and the police advised against a church ceremony, so they were married in the music room of the Crosfields' house at Highgate, observed by Philip de László's 'delicate and vivacious' portrait of Domini Crosfield.[19] The small group present included Kyriakos and Sofoklis and the faithful Klearchos Markantonakis, just back from Chania, where he had travelled specifically to tell Paraskevoula Blum of the impending marriage. They honeymooned for a few days at La Baule, and for the first time in his life Venizelos had no need to worry about money. On 15 October they set out for the United States, to a wildly enthusiastic welcome at New York and Chicago. In California they stayed with a mutual friend, the pianist and Polish nationalist Ignacy Paderewski, at his ranch at Paso Robles. Venizelos knew him from the Peace Conference; he had visited Helena's family years earlier in England. Venizelos played golf at Santa Barbara and was strong rather than accurate: it was best to keep out of his line of fire. They went on to Panama and to Peru, but Helena became ill at Cuzco and their wanderings ended at that point. Back in Paris she bought an apartment for them (22, rue Beaujon, second floor), and her mother settled close at hand at the familiar Hôtel Mercédès.

During their travels the Greater Greece that had consumed so much of Venizelos's political life suffered two severe setbacks. First, Albania (which had joined the League of Nations in December 1920) demanded that its 1913 frontiers should be confirmed. In the face of strong protests led by Nikolaos Politis, now Greek ambassador in Paris, this demand was accepted by the Powers, who thus nullified what had been discussed and decided at Paris in 1919: northern Epirus reverted to Albania.[20] Then, in summer 1922, Italy formally repudiated the Tittoni pact and the 'little treaty of Sèvres'; the Dodecanese would not, after all, be transferred to Greece.

Venizelos was scarcely back in Paris when a third setback came, the most devastating of all. The Greek lines at

Afyonkarahisar were suddenly attacked in force by Turkish troops. On 26 August the Greeks gave way and began a rapid retreat westward. They had no second line of defence, and the retreat turned into a disorderly rout in which tens of thousands of Greek soldiers vied with hundreds of thousands of Greek-speaking inhabitants of the occupied zone to reach Smyrna. There was no refuge for them in Asia. Safety lay across the sea, in Greece or the Aegean islands, and there were too few ships to take them all. The Turkish army advanced on Smyrna with great speed. The barbarism sometimes shown by the Greeks during the last three years (at Aydın and Bursa worse had happened than during the disorderly early days) was now turned back on them; it was the refugee population, crowded into Smyrna and unable to escape in time, who suffered. Smyrna itself, historic centre of Greek culture in Asia Minor, was largely destroyed. Wealthy Greeks in western Europe – Emmanouil Benakis and Helena Venizelos prominent among them – were active almost at once in sending money and supplies to relieve the needs of the Asia Minor refugees, the lucky ones, who had reached Greece. Almost all of them were destitute.

British troops, few in numbers, still guarded the Straits; they alone had the power to dissuade Turkish troops from crossing to Thrace to win back that territory also. It was at Venizelos's suggestion (though he had no official standing) that the secretary at the London embassy, Leon Melas, motored to Harold Nicolson's house near Sevenoaks on Sunday 17 September to find out what the British would do. Nicolson was allowed to assure him privately that they would hold on. It was not Venizelos's fault that this hasty resolution became public, caused a crisis in Britain's relations with its allies and precipitated Lloyd George's fall.[21]

The Greek government was in collapse, and those troops that had reached the Aegean islands in good order decided that it must be replaced. Their Revolutionary Committee was led by Nikolaos Plastiras, a Venizelist since Salonica, a hero of 1918 and of the recent retreat. The ultimatum, demanding the King's immediate abdication, reached Athens on 26 September. The Committee entrusted foreign policy to Venizelos in Paris. He focused his first diplomatic efforts on retaining Eastern Thrace, but it was too late. The armistice agreed on 10 October returned the territory to Turkey.

The peace conference, to be held at Lausanne, would take place in a new political environment. King Constantine had left Greece for the last time; his successor was his eldest son, George II. On 4 November the Caliph at Constantinople was deposed, and Kemal ruled Turkey unchallenged. Eleven days later the Conservatives won the British elections, but Curzon retained the post of Foreign Secretary that he had formerly held in the Lloyd George coalition. As he, Venizelos and others assembled at Lausanne, the Revolutionary Committee in Athens held a show trial at Goudi. On the grounds that they had led Greece into the Asia Minor catastrophe, Gounaris, four other political leaders, and General Chatzanestis faced execution for treason.

Greek political rivalries had never been sharper than in the mortal struggle between Venizelos and Gounaris (who in 1920 possibly had foreknowledge of the plot to kill Venizelos at the Gare de Lyon). Had these strangely similar figures been leaders of neighbouring countries they might well have been friends; in Greece they were irreconcilable. Now, in a telegram to the Committee, Venizelos mildly observed that executions would make his task more difficult. Curzon, more decisive, sent Commander Talbot to Athens to urge clemency. The six were found guilty on 27 November and shot next morning. Talbot arrived too late – but was allowed to escort into exile Constantine's brother, Prince Andrew, who was on trial for insubordination.[22]

Present at Lausanne were the five Supreme Powers from Paris (Britain, France, Italy, Japan and the United States), Turkey, Greece, Bulgaria, Serbia and Romania. Curzon needed to ensure British possession of oil-rich Mosul and international rights of passage through the Straits. He also wanted to isolate the 'arrogant' Turks and to reunite the Allies, who in their recent dealings with Turkey had shown little evidence of alliance. The leader of the Turkish delegation was İsmet (later known as İsmet İnönü). He not only had to assert Turkey's new power but also to begin the task of reconciliation with a defeated Greece and a supercilious and wounded Britain.

Venizelos, Michalakopoulos and Kaklamanos represented Greece. Their task was to rescue what they could from military defeat. Their success is a measure of Venizelos's personal influence as well his negotiating skills. Joseph Grew, who had seen little of him at Paris, eventually led the American delegation and gives a fresh characterisation. Although Venizelos's claims were 'often illogical and frequently inaccurate' he held his audience's attention. Beginning gently, he would gradually 'work himself into a fury ... and wildly wave his arms in the air'. When begged to be tranquil 'Mr. Venizelos beat the table with his fists in redoubled violence and shouted at the top of his lungs: *I am tranquil, I am tranquil* ... His passionate duels across the table with Riza Nour Bey, the Turk, were the delight of the conference.'[23]

Eastern Thrace was lost, he decided. Greece might have fought for it – Army chiefs at home begged to be given a free hand – but she needed peace without border conflicts. The sacrifice mollified Turkey and Bulgaria; with British help the two states were persuaded to relinquish their claims to western Thrace and the Aegean islands.

He had to save the Greeks of the Pontus and the rest of Anatolia – those who still survived and had not already fled to Greece. Venizelos's eastward diplomacy, from December 1912 up to and including the Smyrna discussions at Paris, had always kept in view the lives of over a million Greeks living under Muslim rule (it was clear from recent events and from the fate of the Armenians, still fresh in memory, that their lives were literally at stake). He had one bargaining counter left: the Muslims of Greece. He could draw on precedents in previous agreements, in 1914 with Turkey and in 1919 with Bulgaria. These concerned voluntary exchanges; now Venizelos and İsmet agreed a Greek-Turkish Convention on compulsory population exchange, with compensation on both sides for lost assets. The big Greek community of Constantinople (henceforth Istanbul), seat of the Greek Orthodox Patriarch, was not to be uprooted; the Greek inhabitants of Imbros and Tenedos (Gökçeada and Bozcaada) were also excepted. 'Probably only Venizelos could have negotiated [this agreement] and sold it to the Greek people.'[24]

The wider conference broke up temporarily on 4 February when Curzon swept out of Lausanne on the Orient Express; he missed the second phase. Turkey demanded reparations for the destruction wreaked in Asia Minor during the three years of fighting; Greece could not pay. To the last week it was uncertain whether a treaty would be signed. In early May Venizelos was threatening a military attack on Eastern Thrace if Turkey stood firm. Finally, on 26 May, there was a strictly private and 'intensely dramatic' meeting chaired by Pellé, the French delegate, to discuss his suggestion that Turkey should accept the district of Karagac, on the border between western and eastern Thrace, in lieu of reparations. 'We all sat close together at a small table,' Grew recalled; Diamandy, the Romanian, 'placed himself between İsmet and Venizelos with a view to separating the principals in the controversy.' After two hours of dogged argument İsmet finally admitted that he had been authorised by telegram to agree. 'The air of solemnity changed immediately into one bordering on actual hilarity. Diamandy got up and insisted upon Venizelos moving next to İsmet. The details of the settlement were then discussed in the most amicable way; Venizelos and İsmet calling each other *mon cher ami* had their hands on each other's arms, laughed like school boys, and appeared to be on the point of actually embracing ... Rumbold, the Englishman, showed his wild enthusiasm by a contraction of the facial muscles which amounted almost to a smile.'[25] Alexandris and Kaklamanos were among those waiting anxiously outside: 'At about 6 p.m., emerging first with big strides, and beaming with joy, Venizelos said to the waiting journalists – *Messieurs! C'est la paix!*'[26]

The paradoxical formula that permitted agreement at Lausanne was drafted by Venizelos himself. *Greece recognises her obligation to make reparation for the damage caused in Anatolia by the acts of the Greek army or administration which were contrary to the laws of war, and ... Turkey, in consideration of the financial situation of Greece resulting from the prolongation of the war and from its consequences, finally renounces all claims for reparation.*[27]

Thus the negotiations begun in 1919 were at last concluded. At Paris Venizelos thought he had gained Asia Minor, soon lost in war; northern Epirus, reclaimed by Albania two years later; and the Dodecanese, which Italy kept after all. The aftermath saw the Greek annexation of eastern Thrace, now sacrificed at Lausanne, and western Thrace, solidly Greek to this day. The poisoned prize had been Asia Minor, which opportunism and optimism impelled Venizelos to accept, aware that the occupation of Smyrna was 'the last and only realistic plan' to save the Greek communities and cultures of Anatolia from destruction.[28] The plan failed.

Venizelos with the Turkish Prime Minister İsmet İnönü (left) in the early 1930s.

III

The Legacy

8

Venizelos's Later Career

The Treaty of Lausanne was signed on 24 July 1923 and Venizelos was free to return to Paris; but his weak response to the trial at Goudi was a sign, for those who could read it, that he still had ambitions in Athens.

In his absence the radical left of the Liberal Party, led by Alexandros Papanastasiou, had found a separate identity as the Republican Union (eventually, in 1926, to become the Farmer-Labour Party). On the other side of the spectrum Ioannis Metaxas attempted an anti-Venizelist counter-revolution in October 1923, after which George II was compelled to go into exile; in a subsequent referendum 70 per cent were to vote for a republic. Through all this the Liberal Party, cleansed by its exclusion from politics during the catastrophe and potentially in command of the centre ground, never replaced its absent hero. Venizelos had not let go the reins; as Michalakopoulos said to Danglis, the caretaker leader, 'It's unlucky for Greece that no organisation not expressly recognised by him has any authority, at home or abroad. His personality exerted overwhelming power, and it still does.'[1] Few, then, were surprised that at Christmas Venizelos wrote to Plastiras announcing his return to help to solve the political crisis. He sailed from Marseille to Piraeus and took over as Prime Minister from Plastiras's colleague Stylianos Gonatas. But it would not stick. The Liberals would not unite. After three weeks he gave way to his Justice Minister, formerly envoy of the Salonica government, Georgios Kafandaris. At least once it was reported that Venizelos had collapsed in the Chamber during the fiery debates of that chaotic period. Within two months he had returned to exile, defeated.

His departure (and Danglis's sudden death) left the Liberals in greater disarray. They split three ways, the 'conservatives' under Michalakopoulos, the centre under Themistoklis Sofoulis, the 'progressives' under Kafandaris, who meanwhile gave way to Papanastasiou as Prime Minister. Meanwhile Gounaris's Popular Party, after the trauma of his execution, was led by the indecisive Panagis Tsaldaris. Three more years of political strife culminated in the brief and incompetent dictatorship of Theodoros Pangalos – who as a young army officer in 1909 had been among the first to talk of inviting Venizelos to Athens.

In Paris on 2 August 1924 Venizelos's first grandson, Kyriakos' son, was born and named Eleftherios after his grandfather, who now dedicated himself to a project that seems very different from the politics on which he had spent his life, but followed naturally enough: the translation into modern Greek of Thucydides' *History of the Peloponnesian War*, the first classic of political history.

He completed the translation but never saw it published. It appeared in Britain, under Kaklamanos's editorship, in 1937–40, and never became really popular in Greece. However liberally he favoured the proponents of demotic Greek, Venizelos was a classicist at heart, and his translated Thucydides was tied to the archaic grammar of the original. Alongside the translation he wrote a commentary in separate notebooks. All too brief, it notes a few analogies between politics in the 5th century BC and the 20th century AD. When the Thebans defend themselves for having chosen the wrong side in the Persian war of 480 BC with the explanation that their government at the time was undemocratic, Venizelos remarks drily that *the same arguments were put forward to the Peace Conference after the Great War by Turkish and Bulgarian delegates to save their countries from the consequences of the policies they had followed*.[2] When the Athenian demagogue Cleon praises his fellow citizens for being 'excellent not only at falling for new ideas but also at refusing sensible advice, slaves as you are to each new paradox'. Venizelos acidly observes the *bitter irony*, adding: *the oddest thing is that it should be Cleon who insists on this*. Cleon, like many in modern Athenian politics, was excellent at selling new and unwise policies to his audiences.[3]

Helena Venizelos's philanthropy focused on relieving suffering and poverty among the vast refugee population of Greece; but in her husband's native Chania the Cretan Fine Arts Union, led by a dedicated demoticist, the young musician Manolis Skouloudis, thought it worth writing to Venizelos to ask for money for a conservatory. The union's secretary was Kostis Foumis, Venizelos's ally long ago, who stood against him in the 1910 elections in Greece and had been his enemy ever since. *Seeing your signature moved me very deeply*, Venizelos replied to Foumis,[4] and, sure enough, Helena paid for the concert hall, which is still in use today. An even greater benefaction was a new maternity hospital on the edge of Athens with a view of Mount Hymettus. Begun in 1927 and completed in 1933, it is now the Elena Venizelos

Hospital. As these contacts show, Venizelos could not break free from Greece. In spring 1927 he returned once more to Piraeus (but saw no one there) and continued to Chania, where Helena bought new furniture for the house in Chalepa built by his father in 1880, the house that ever since 1906 he had had to let to tenants to make ends meet. She also raised the roof by about a metre; it now overshadows Prince George's crumbling palace. She lived there sometimes, but she was in Paris when, on 6 May 1928, he wrote with the news that he had been asked by Alexandros Diomidis to become President of Greece. *If the people decide <u>by a substantial majority</u> to summon me to the highest office, morally I cannot refuse the duty.*[5]

This was a red herring; as it turned out, the Presidency was not available. Nor was the Premiership; the current coalition government was led, for the last time in a life of compromises, by Alexandros Zaimis (soon to succeed Koundouriotis as President). The Progressive Liberals, however, wanted a leader. Georgios Kafandaris chafed at the volume of advice from Venizelos that rendered him no more than a caretaker; he resigned, and Venizelos filled the vacancy, claiming to friends that he did so to forestall a military coup (which he had toyed with supporting). Speaking at the Liberal Club he disingenuously urged the other parties *to endorse democratic government, under the condition, if they so choose, that I resign this Liberal leadership, even that I leave the country again and, if it comes to that, die in exile.*[6] In truth he foresaw a different future, and on 3 July became Prime Minister for the fifth time in preparation for elections in August in which the resurgent Liberals, with the help of electoral juggling, took 178 out of 250 seats. The Cabinet included a young Georgios Papandreou – eventually Education Minister

– alongside old allies such as Michalakopoulos and Alexandris. The journalist Georgios Vlachos wrote in the Athens daily *Kathimerini* that Venizelos's victory meant the political dictatorship of the Liberals and the economic dictatorship of the refugees;[7] it meant, at all events, a full four years of Venizelist government, broadly-based at first, narrowing in response to party disputes.

There was plenty to do. Under Papandreou the Education Ministry built 3,167 schools, made co-education the norm, gave unobtrusive support to *dimotiki* and reformed the secondary syllabus, which was henceforth less classical and more vocational. On the economic front urgent aims were to increase agricultural production, shifting from export crops to wheat, of which there was never enough; following from this, to expand the market for local trade and industry, which would then benefit from the vastly increased labour pool. All this meant generous investment in infrastructure financed by generous foreign loans. Guided by the new Bank of Greece it might have worked, assuming stability in the world economy. The plan was overtaken by the international economic crash, to which Greece was slow to react, disastrously attempting to stay on the gold standard when Britain abandoned it. Venizelos's diplomatic skills helped in rescheduling existing loans but not in arranging new ones.

His surest achievement during these four years was in foreign policy. He found Greece on poor terms with her neighbours and set out to change this. First came Italy. However much she wanted the Dodecanese, Greece could gain nothing by treating Italy as an enemy. He had to tread carefully. Mussolini offered a defensive alliance and a guarantee to protect Salonica against attack; Venizelos refused because Belgrade and Paris would see any such agreement as potentially threatening. *They will certainly not believe that Italy gave this guarantee without asking anything from Greece in return … I will have to tell them about the guarantee, because that's the way I operate in politics: I will have to say 'Mr Mussolini has given me this guarantee', and they will suspect some more extensive alliance between us. This is why I said that, to my distress, I must refuse.* Venizelos and Mussolini signed a pact of friendship, and *since that day, in every case where we needed Italy's support, it was accorded without any reservation.*[8]

Yugoslavia was the second focus. Here a pointless dispute over the railway and port facilities at Salonica was soon settled, leading to a bilateral cooperation agreement in March 1929.

As early as August 1928 Venizelos had written to his friend İsmet, in Ankara, proposing a treaty of friendship. This led to Venizelos's visit to Turkey in October 1930 to sign a friendship and neutrality agreement. Greece made concessions over reparation issues but gained economically because the costly arms race ended. Helena, familiar with Asia Minor from her childhood, accompanied him, noting that Turkish women, no longer veiled, now wore high heels and went into tea shops. Atatürk danced with her (Greek friends told her she should have refused) and gave her two white angora cats.

With Venizelos's support the National Gallery in Athens in 1931 bought El Greco's 'Concert of the Angels' at auction in Munich; the Gallery's long-serving director, Zacharias Papantoniou, a Venizelos appointment in 1918, continued throughout the economic crisis to channel government support to contemporary Greek artists. The Greek National Theatre was founded, and his enthusiasm for Greek culture led him in January 1931 to the basement of an Athens theatre

where he sang two Cretan ballads for Melpo Merlier's eth-
nomusicology project, begun with the aim of preserving the
disappearing folk music of the Greek refugees from Asia
Minor. The newspapers had a field day with 'Greece's most
famous tenor'; the recordings survive.[9]

As the crisis deepened the government's popularity faltered. Any stick would do to beat Venizelos, and any compromises appeared wilful failure to defend Greek interests.
As Tache Ionescu wrote presciently in 1915, 'His actions
were closely watched at Athens. Every concession this great
man made to the peace of Europe and the security of Greece
was made the occasion of attacking him as a weakling who
had no faith in the power of Hellenism.'[10] In 1929 Cyprus
exemplified this. Alexis Kyrou, the Greek Consul-General
in Nikosia, had encouraged the island's Greek nationalists.
Venizelos's immediate insistence that Greek interests dictated
close friendship with Britain, and in 1931 his firm condem-
nation of the Cyprus uprising, played well with Britain but
badly at home. His charisma had begun to fail him. 'We have
Venizelos, Venizelos's nerves, Venizelos's moods, Venizelos's
anger, Venizelos's humour, Venizelos's punishments, and the
blue-and-white flag above it all,' Georgios Vlachos argued in
Kathimerini in 1931, 'but do they add up to a form of government?'[11] That year saw a succession of ministerial scandals
and a series of bad by-elections: the Asia Minor refugees,
disillusioned by the concessions in Ankara, wavered in their
support for Venizelos and the Liberals, turning in significant
numbers to Communism.

Venizelos was now living far more grandly than in earlier
years, at the Petit Palais that had once been Prince Nicholas's
house, but it was rented accommodation still. Helena now
began to build a house on Loukianou Street that would be big

enough for a political leader's entertaining. It was completed in 1932 with the traditional killing of a cock. Venizelos, who thought this rite barbaric, perhaps never knew that it had taken place.[12] They were to live there for scarcely a year.

After a faltering campaign the Venizelists came out of the 1932 election badly. The Venizelist parties had a tiny majority (131 out of 250) if counted together, but in fact they could not unite. Tsaldaris, as Popular Party leader, recognised the Republican constitution (a step he had long refused to take) and formed a cabinet, of which Ioannis Metaxas, after many years of small-party independence, became a member. But Tsaldaris's minority government relied on Liberal votes, and the following January the Liberals brought it down: they had agreed, briefly, on a united front led by Venizelos and supported by his strayed allies Papanastasiou and Kafandaris. The Venizelist government survived for the seven weeks until new elections were held, but lost decisively. Tsaldaris took power once again. Venizelos's military ally, Nikolaos Plastiras, found this result unacceptable and attempted a coup; then, lacking adequate support, fled to Italy. Venizelos was fiercely criticised for supporting him (there is no sure evidence that he did) and when he next spoke in the Chamber, tactlessly insisting on Plastiras's 'great services' to Greece, was shouted down. It was his last appearance there. *I would be happy*, he had said in spring 1932, *if I were to depart on my longest journey after restoring to Greece the unity that was lost in our national schism, to which I, among others, contributed*;[13] his actions during these 12 months (like those of his opponents) sharpened the division.

'His greatness offended people in a way one could hardly imagine.'
TACHE IONESCU[14]

On 6 June Venizelos, Helena and some of his staff drove to

Kifisia, 15 kilometres north of Athens, to dine with the Deltas. As they returned, towards midnight, an 'American car' pulled out between the two vehicles of the Venizelos party and shots were fired. There was a chase lasting 20 minutes. Helena was hit twice and one of Venizelos's staff, in the car behind, was killed. Their driver, though hit in the arm, managed to get them to Evangelismos Hospital. It is confidently claimed that the new security police chief, Ioannis Polychronopoulos, a Tsaldaris appointment, organised this assassination attempt. Outraged by the half-hearted enquiries that followed, Venizelos retired to Crete, reasonably claiming that he and Helena were no longer safe in Athens. In the autumn Tsaldaris proposed to him that both investigations, those of the Plastiras coup and the attempted assassination, should be shelved, but this bargain he contemptuously rejected. At length, in late 1934, writing from Crete (with research help from Kyriakos, who collected information for him at the Quai d'Orsay) he began a series of articles for an Athenian newspaper, rehearsing the politics of the national schism and warning of future civil war. Metaxas, for 20 years his enemy, began a series in reply; thus 'the former premier and the future dictator fought out the First World War all over again in the pages of the Athens press'.[15] Athens was awash with rumours of coups and dictatorships.

And indeed on 1 March 1935 another coup was attempted, this time by retired and dismissed Venizelist army officers, supposedly aiming to forestall a right-wing revolution and the King's recall. It was as inefficient and abortive as that of 1933. Plastiras was again involved (but Italy would not allow him to leave); this time, so was Venizelos. Greece asked for aircraft from Britain and France to help maintain order. In a last throw for their old ally, both countries refused, to their subsequent embarrassment. Venizelos set out optimistically from Crete for Piraeus. Learning *en route* that Metaxas in Athens had already suppressed the revolt, he returned to Crete and from there, with Helena, hastily fled to Kasos, the nearest island of the Dodecanese, where they stayed overnight in a monastery; their friend Mussolini (who had not supported the coup) arranged for them to go on to Rhodes and by ferry to Naples. There, it seems, Venizelos suffered a minor stroke.

> 'I have a worm inside me: the national schism torments me. Before I die, I want to see Greece united in spirit, as she was in 1912.'
>
> **VENIZELOS IN 1936**

He and Plastiras were now sentenced to death in absentia, and Kyriakos (whose activities at the Quai d'Orsay were perhaps not limited to historical research) to ten years' imprisonment; the new house in Athens was confiscated. Venizelos and Helena settled once more in Paris. Letters still arrived demanding his return, and he was strongly tempted.

Venizelos always suffered from *skoutoures*, 'black thoughts', and (so he told Penelope Delta) he would re-read her hilarious *Trelantonis* to exorcize them.[16] As a result of such wakeful hours, when asked his mistakes he always had answers ready. He was wrong to have chosen Prince Alexander in 1917, passing over Prince George;[17] he was wrong to have hurriedly asked Paul to succeed when Alexander died, and wrong not to postpone the elections when Paul refused;[18] he was wrong to have returned to Athens in 1917 guarded by French bayonets. The biggest error, though it was not his alone, had been made earlier still: *Listen,* he said in early 1936 to a visitor, a friend and journalist, *I'll tell you a secret. I have a worm inside me: the national schism torments me ...*

it has lasted far too long, and it is high time to put an end to it. Before I die, I want to see Greece united in spirit, as she was in 1912 and 1913.[19] In these last months there seemed some chance that this would be achieved. On 3 November 1935 a referendum recalled George II to Greece, and Venizelos (omitting to notice that Sofoulis had succeeded him as Liberal leader) wrote instructing the Party to recognise the King as head of state. Not long afterwards George proclaimed an amnesty, revoking the death sentence on Venizelos and formally restoring his ownership of the house in Athens. *Long live the King!* wrote Venizelos in one of his last letters,[20] and in a message to a Cretan school friend, Giankos Iliakis, promised to return later in the year – but he would be too late to harvest his plums and apricots; Iliakis himself would have to eat them.[21]

On the Paris newsstands on the morning of 13 March 1936 *L'Intransigeant* headlined a gloomy interview with Venizelos. His message was that the League of Nations that he had helped to found was powerless. *We have returned to prewar conditions. Every country is forced to arm as fast and as heavily as it can; every country has to form military alliances. The Rhineland coup shows that no one can be sure any longer of security at home or of peace in Europe.*[22] That same morning Helena found him in his bedroom, standing, his eyes fixed, his mouth sagging to the right. He did not reply to her questions. She steered him to bed and telephoned his sons and a specialist, who diagnosed a stroke. His right side became paralysed and his speech became indistinct. For four days he hovered in and out of touch with the world, though able to recognise Vasilios Skoulas, his old friend and doctor. He died on the morning of the 18th, gripping Helena's hand.

There were two religious ceremonies, one in the Armenian

church and one in the Greek church on rue Georges-Bizet, at which Apostolos Alexandris, Venizelos's friend and collaborator since 1910, spoke at length, reminding the dead man of 'the unimaginable circumstances in which you struggled to realize your plan for Greece; the enmity of Italy … the obstinate insistence of President Wilson, to the very moment of his death, that Thrace should not be awarded to Greece.'[23] There were military honours at the Gare de Lyon, scene of the 1920 shooting. The body travelled by train to Brindisi, thence in the warship *Averoff* to Chania, where it lay for two nights in the church of Mary Magdalene at Chalepa while black-robed women mourners lamented noisily. The final ceremony, on 29 March, was on Profitis Ilias Hill, where, 39 years earlier, the revolutionaries of Akrotiri had raised the flag of Greece. Soon afterwards a memorial slab was placed there, commanding a spectacular view of Chania and Chalepa. Far below, quite unmistakeable, in precise alignment with the stone, rises the gable of the Venizelos house, with Prince George's palace just visible behind.

Helena says she took the decision that the *Averoff* should not call at Piraeus and afterwards regretted it when she saw the flowers massed before their Athens house. She sold the house to the British government and it became the embassy residence. She eventually sold the Paris apartment, dropped her police protection and lived at the Hôtel George V. She died in 1959. Kyriakos, an international businessman more often seen in France and the United States than in Greece, died of a heart attack in 1942. Sofoklis, having followed his father into liberal politics, was three times Prime Minister of Greece between 1944 and 1951; he died in 1964 and was buried beside his father. Throngs of tourists and schoolchildren now gather around the 'Venizelos Graves'. Sofoklis' son

Nikitas, in turn, has been a prominent Liberal and a European MP. There is irony here. Venizelos's opposition to the old personal parties of Greece went back to his student days, and in 1910 he believed he was a flag-bearer for new political ideas, yet the new Liberal Party was as tied to personality as its rivals. Its link with its leader was not broken by his exile in 1920, nor by his renewed exile and death sentence in 1935 – not even by his death.

The confusion that was Greek political life was temporarily silenced, in the very year of Venizelos's death, by a method that he would not have approved. Ioannis Metaxas, once Venizelos's aide-de-camp, became Prime Minister in April and with the acquiescence of King George II established a dictatorship in August. He tried to retain British and German friendship while resisting the threat from Mussolini's Italy, which eventually invaded across the Albanian border in October 1940. Greece counter-attacked successfully, even occupying northern Epirus. Metaxas died that winter and therefore did not witness the inevitable sequel. Mussolini appealed to Hitler; Italian fortunes revived when German troops invaded Greece by way of Bulgaria in April 1941, rapidly occupying the whole country, including Crete, where British and Commonwealth troops had vainly attempted to dig in. Ioannis Rallis, son of Dimitrios, was one of the Prime Ministers of occupied Greece (he died in prison in 1946). Sofoklis Venizelos and Georgios Papandreou were among the leaders

> 'Venizelos is dead, and along with him we are all dead: Venizelists, anti-Venizelists; the past, the political camps.'
> GEORGIOS VLACHOS[24]

of the government in exile at Cairo. The occupiers were driven out in 1944. The Greek resistance, however, fed into an increasingly powerful Communist movement (already outlawed under Venizelos and Metaxas), which fought a bitter civil war until 1949.

The influential journalist Georgios Vlachos thought that the National Schism would end with Venizelos's death. He was wrong, of course. Even the civil war did not end it. It took a second dictatorship, that of the Colonels, to demonstrate that reconciliation was the only possible route; it took the two following governments to achieve it. These were led successively by the Conservatives Konstantinos Karamanlis and Georgios Rallis (son of Ioannis), and the socialist Andreas Papandreou (son of Georgios). Greece still has its political families.

On the map of Greece's frontiers no revision occurred for more than 20 years after the Treaty of Lausanne. At last the collapse of Fascist Italy in 1943 heralded change. German troops conquered the Dodecanese and held the islands until 1945, when a British military protectorate was imposed. After another Paris Peace Conference, formally ending hostilities between the Allies and Italy, the islands of the Dodecanese were transferred to Greece in 1947. Meanwhile Cyprus, which Venizelos had hoped to receive from Britain as a *beau geste*, remained a British colony until 1960, shaken by ethnic tension and violence. In that year the island became independent. A coup in 1974, encouraged by the Greek Colonels, led to a Turkish invasion, compulsory population exchanges, and the continuing division of the island between Greek and Turkish zones. Cyprus reflects, in a distorting mirror, the recent history of Greece and Turkey.

By 1914, in correspondence with Tache Ionescu, Venizelos was hypothesising that the Greeks of the diaspora would eventually migrate towards an enlarged Greece. He had watched the Muslim population of Crete dwindle; he had seen some of the results of the guerilla war in Macedonia; he had personally negotiated population exchanges with Bulgaria and the Ottoman Empire. As he foresaw, the 20th century was to see many more such movements. Greek military participation in 1919 in the disastrous French campaign in the Ukraine would lead to the flight of tens of thousands of Greeks from the northern shores of the Black Sea; Penelope Delta's collections helped to preserve the oral history of the Macedonia and Ukraine campaigns and their aftermaths. Deaths and compulsory migrations after the Asia Minor catastrophe would end the long history of Greek communities in Pontus, Cappadocia and western Asia Minor; the folklore work of Melpo Merlier and her colleagues (for whom Venizelos sang Cretan songs) was originally designed to record the disappearing traditions of the Greeks of Anatolia. As they were scattered, divided and relocated, their culture was consigned to mere libraries and museums, but at least it was preserved. This, too, is part of the legacy of Venizelos.

Notes

Prologue

1. Compton Mackenzie, *Greek Memories* (London: 1932) pp 112–13.
2. H Nicolson, *Peacemaking 1919* (Constable, London: 1933) p 271. Nicolson introduces Talbot as 'the "friend of Venizelos"' (p 246: his inverted commas).
3. N Petsalis-Diomidis, *Greece at the Paris Peace Conference (1919)* (Institute for Balkan Studies, Salonica: 1978) lists 19 members of the delegation. Membership fluctuated; at least 10 names can be added from other authorities.
4. 'What is not generally known is that the Cretan, in the mountains, had books in his pockets, and was using them to complete his French studies' (Take Jonescu, *Some Personal Impressions* [London: 1919] Part 1, Chapter 7).
5. Direct quotations in this paragraph are from Nicolson's diary as printed in Nicolson, *Peacemaking*, p 251.

1: A Revolutionary by Profession

1. Grigorios Dafnis, *Sofoklis Eleftheriou Venizelos* (Ikaros, Athens: 1970) pp 5–6; Lili Makraki, *Eleftherios Venizelos 1864–1910: i diaplasi enos ethnikou igeti* (Athens: 1992) pp 100–1, hereafter Makraki, *Venizelos.* The supposed original letter of 1899 does not survive. This copy was first published (in Greek) in 1929.

2. For example, Kyriakos Venizelos to Markos Renieris, 27 November 1877 (N Polychronopoulos-Kladas, *Istoriko archio Eleftheriou Venizelou* [Idryma Istorias tou Eleftheriou Venizelou, Athens: 2004] item I/2/1).

3. This story was not published in Greek in Venizelos's lifetime, but it did appear in English (first in S B Chester, *Life of Venizelos* [Constable, London: 1921] p 3). Makraki, *Venizelos,* pp 121–2 and S A Apostolakis, *Laografika meletimata gia ton Elefth. K. Venizelo* (Chania: 1995) p 51, accept it as probable.

4. Jules Ballot, *Histoire de l'insurrection crétoise* (Dentu, Paris: 1868) p 322.

5. Letter of 13/25 March 1878 (text in Makraki, *Venizelos,* pp 135–6).

6. Undated letter by Venizelos and reply of 26 July/7 August 1879 by Kyriakos; text in K Mitsotakis, *Ta mikra chronia enos megalou* (Athens: 1972) pp 53–63.

7. Royal *Gymnasion*, Syros, 28 June/10 July 1880; University of Athens, 8/20 October 1880 (N Polychronopoulos-Kladas, *Istoriko archio Eleftheriou Venizelou* [Idryma Istorias tou Eleftheriou Venizelou, Athens: 2004] item I/3/1–2); Georgios Vendiris, *I Ellas tou 1910–1920: istoriki meleti* (Athens: 1931) Vol 1, p 53, hereafter Vendiris, *I Ellas*; University of Athens, 8/20

October 1882: kapodistriako.uoa.gr/stories/073_hi_01/index.php?m=2, retrieved 5 May 2008.

8. Letter of 6/18 March 1883 (text in Makraki, *Venizelos*, pp 159–60).

9. *New York Times* (8 June 1886) p 1.

10. Full text of the interview in Ioannis G Manolikakis (ed), *Eleftheriou Venizelou: I Kritiki epanastasis tou 1889* (Athens: 1971) pp 26–32; compare the translation in Doros Alastos, *Venizelos, Patriot, Statesman, Revolutionary* (Lund Humphries, London: 1942) pp 14–18, hereafter Alastos, *Venizelos*.

11. Gryparis to Stefanos Dragoumis, 4/16 May 1889 (quoted in Makraki, *Venizelos*, p 234).

12. Memoir by Foumis in the unpublished 'Akrotiri Diary' (quoted in Makraki, *Venizelos*, p 270; English summary in A Lilly Macrakis, 'Venizelos' Early Life and Political Career in Crete, 1864–1910' in Paschalis M Kitromilides (ed), *Eleftherios Venizelos: the trials of statesmanship* [Edinburgh University Press, Edinburgh: 2006] p 55); Giannis Mourellos, *Venizelos: i agapes tou, i chares tou, i odynes tou* (Athens: 1964) pp 111–12, hereafter Mourellos, *Venizelos*.

13. Ioannis G Manolikakis (ed), *Eleftheriou Venizelou: I Kritiki epanastasis tou 1889* (Athens: 1971).

14. Charalambos Bournazos cited at www.venizelos-foundation.gr/endocs/biomid.jsp (retrieved 30 November 2007).

15. Letter to the Admirals, 10/22 February 1897, from the 'Akrotiri Diary' (text in Giannis Manolikakis, *Eleftherios Venizelos: i agnosti zoi tou* [Gnosi, Athens: 1985] p 148, hereafter Manolikakis, *Venizelos*).

16. Letter to the Admirals, 15/27 February 1897 (text in Makraki, *Venizelos*, p 357).

17. H A Gibbons, *Venizelos* (T Fisher Unwin, London: 1921) pp 26–7, citing the unnamed officer's 'letter home'.

18. Kostas Kairofylas, *Eleftherios Venizelos: his life and work* (London: 1915) pp 21–4; Vendiris, *I Ellas*, Vol 1 pp 48–9.

19. Text in S A Papantonakis, *Kritika* (Chania: 1901) p 18.

2: Princely Crete

1. He used this phrase in a speech to the foreign press at a banquet in his honour, Paris, 1919 (reported in Gibbons, *Venizelos*, pp 37–8).

2. E S Bagger, *Eminent Europeans* (Putnam, New York: 1922) pp 69–70. Or maybe 'I intend to govern Crete like Peter the Great' (V Gavriilidis as quoted in A A Pallis (ed), *The Cretan Drama: the life and memoirs of Prince George of Greece, High Commissioner in Crete (1898–1906)* [New York: 1959] p 267); or 'Gentlemen, you should know that I came here to rule à la Grand Pierre' (Mourellos, *Venizelos*, p 147; Alastos, *Venizelos*, p 39).

3. Bagger, *Eminent Europeans*, p 70; similarly Alastos, *Venizelos*, p 39.

4. Vlasis Gavriilidis (cited in Pallis (ed), *The Cretan Drama*, p 268), reporting a 1905 interview, stated that the Prince proposed the scheme; George himself, writing many years later (Pallis (ed), *The Cretan Drama*, pp 39–41, cf. p 179) claims that Venizelos proposed it, and that he unwillingly accepted it.

5. Biliotti to Sir Thomas Sanderson, 28 January 1889 (quoted in R F Holland, 'Nationalism, Ethnicity

and the Concert of Europe: the case of the High Commissionership of Prince George of Greece in Crete, 1898–1906', *Journal of Modern Greek Studies* 17 (1999) pp 253–76 at p 256, hereafter Holland, 'Nationalism').

6. Pallis (ed), *The Cretan Drama*, pp 73–4.

7. Conversation with N Avraam, recounted in an article by K N Avraam in 1936 (adjusted from the translation in A Lilly Macrakis, 'Venizelos' Early Life and Political Career in Crete, 1864–1910' in Kitromilides (ed), *Venizelos,* p 70).

8. Pallis (ed), *The Cretan Drama*, p 97.

9. Pallis (ed), *The Cretan Drama,* pp 99–100.

10. Pallis (ed), *The Cretan Drama,* p 128.

11. Pallis (ed), *The Cretan Drama*, p 243.

12. V Gavriilidis quoted in Pallis (ed), *The Cretan Drama*, p 269.

13. Graves to Lord Lansdowne, 11 March 1903 (quoted in Holland, 'Nationalism', p 260).

14. Memorandum by Esme Howard, 14 July 1904 (quoted in Holland, 'Nationalism', p 260).

15. Pallis (ed), *The Cretan Drama*, p 284.

16. Venizelos to his sons, 28 September/11 October 1906 (text in Dafnis, *Sofoklis Venizelos*, p 20).

17. Mourellos, *Venizelos*, p 158; Manolikakis, *Venizelos*, p 37.

18. Reported in Kairofylas, *Eleftherios Venizelos*, p 48.

19. In parliamentary debate on 15 March 1913. S I Stefanou (ed), *Ta kimena tou Eleftheriou Venizelou, 1909–1935*, 4 vols (Leschi Fileleftheron, Athens: 1981–1984) Vol 1, p 417, hereafter Stefanou (ed), *Kimena*; Mark Mazower, 'The Messiah and the Bourgeoisie: Venizelos and Politics

in Greece, 1909–1912', *Historical Journal*, 35 (1992) pp 885–904 at p 897, hereafter Mazower, 'Messiah'.

20. Theodoros Pangalos, *Ta apomnimonevmata mou* (Kedros, Athens: 1959) Vol 1, pp 47–8. Passaris was to be Air Minister under the Metaxas dictatorship.

3: Liberal Greece

1. *Kiryx* (26 August/8 September 1909); text in Stefanou (ed), *Kimena*, Vol 1, pp 143–5; compare the translation in Helen Gardikas-Katsiadakis, 'Venizelos' Advent in Greek Politics, 1909–12' in Kitromilides (ed), *Venizelos*, pp 90–1.

2. Letter by Venizelos afterwards published in *Neos Kosmos* (25 December 1933).

3. *The Times* (London, 15 February 1910) p 5.

4. Elliot to Grey, 31 January 1910 (quoted in S Victor Papacosma, *The Military in Greek Politics: the 1909 coup d'état* [Kent State University Press: 1997] p 123).

5. *The Times* (London, 4 February 1910) p 5.

6. E F B Grogan, *Life of J D Bourchier* (London: 1926) p 136; *The Times* (London, 16 February 1910) p 9.

7. *The Times* (London, 22 August 1910) p 5; Helen Gardikas-Katsiadakis, 'Venizelos' Advent in Greek Politics, 1909–12' in Kitromilides (ed), *Venizelos*, pp 95–6.

8. Joachim G Joachim, *Ioannis Metaxas: the formative years, 1871–1922* (Bibliopolis, Mannheim: 2000) p 81, hereafter Joachim, *Metaxas*.

9. *The Times* (London, 4 April 1910) p 5.

10. *Neon Asty* ('New City', 24 August 1910, as quoted by George Mavrogordatos, *Stillborn Republic: social conditions and party strategy in Greece 1922–1936*

[University of California Press, Berkeley: 1983] p 66); *The Times* (London, 22 August and 5 September 1910).

11. *The Times* (London, 25 August 1910) p 3.

12. *The Times* (London, 4 April and 15 September 1910); Apostolos Alexandris, *Politike anamnisis* (Patras: 1947) p 39.

13. Text in Stefanou, *Kimena*, Vol 1 pp 174–8; compare the translations in Mazower, 'Messiah', pp 898–9 and at www.venizelos-foundation.gr/endocs/bio06–10_10.jsp (retrieved 13 December 2007).

14. Sources differ even in such details: Metaxas's diary records that he was in the washroom at the time (Apostolos Alexandris, *Politike anamnisis* [Patras: 1947] pp 130–2; Joachim, *Metaxas*, pp 58–62).

15. Papacosma, *The Military in Greek Politics*, p 161.

16. Vendiris, *I Ellas,* esp. Vol 1, pp 70–85.

17. Mavrogordatos, *Stillborn Republic*, pp 121–7; Mazower, 'Messiah'.

18. Joachim, *Metaxas,* p 64.

19. Joachim, *Metaxas,* pp 71–2.

20. As reported by Venizelos to Metaxas (Joachim, *Metaxas*, pp 82–3).

21. Bourchier's record of these negotiations appears in *The Times* (London, 4–16 June 1919) and in Grogan, *Bourchier*, pp 135–42. See also Reginald Rankin, *Inner History of the Balkan War* (London: 1914) and Venizelos's own reminiscence in Grogan, *Bourchier*, pp 215–17.

22. Jonescu, *Some Personal Impressions*, p 243.

23. Theodoros Pangalos, *Ta apomnimonevmata mou* (Kedros, Athens: 1959) Vol 1, pp 182–3; Joachim, *Metaxas*, pp 101–11.

24. *The Times* (London, 9 December 1912) p 7.
25. Irene Noel to Churchill, 7 December 1912 (Churchill Archive, Cambridge).
26. Theodoros P Petrakopoulos, *I zoi mou* (Athens: 1961) p 98.
27. Kairofylas, *Eleftherios Venizelos*, pp 118–20.
28. Kairofylas, *Eleftherios Venizelos*, p 168.
29. P Danglis, *Archion* (Athens: 1965) Vol 1, pp 60–7; Compton Mackenzie, *First Athenian Memories* (Cassell, London: 1931) p 25; Geoffrey Miller, *Superior Force: The Conspiracy Behind the Escape of Goeben and Breslau* [www.manorhouse.clara.net/book1/contents.htm] Ch. 9.
30. Mourellos, *Venizelos*, pp 185–7.

4: The National Schism

1. Vendiris, *I Ellas*, Vol 1, p 261.
2. Miller, *Superior Force*, Ch. 10.
3. Erskine to Grey, 5 August 1914 (quoted by Miller, *Superior Force*, Ch. 11).
4. Reported by Vendiris, *I Ellas*, Vol 1, p 49.
5. On this celebrated incident see now Miller (*Superior Force,* Ch. 11–12) quoting Erskine to Grey, 9 August 1914, and other documents. It is not clear whether Venizelos knew the vessels were bound for Constantinople.
6. Venizelos to Psychas (Greek Minister in Bucharest), undated (Greek text and French translation in Dimitris Michalopoulos, *Attitudes parallèles: Eleutherios Veniselos et Take Ionescu dans la Grande Guerre* [Idryma Istorias tou Eleftheriou Venizelou, Athens:

2004] pp 20–2, 27–8). Serbia was to gain Bosnia, Croatia and Slovenia; Romania was to gain Transylvania.

7. Edward Grey to Francis Elliot, 23 January 1915; Michael Llewellyn Smith, *Ionian Vision: Greece in Asia Minor, 1919–1922* (Allen Lane, London: 1973) pp 35–6. The phrase is often cited in the form *very considerable territorial compensations* as it appears in *The Vindication of Greek National Policy, 1912–1917: a report of speeches delivered in the Greek chamber, August 23 to 26, 1917, by Mr E Venizelos and others, with an introduction by J Gennadius* (Allen & Unwin, London: 1918) p 80, hereafter *Vindication*.

8. In a letter to King Constantine on 17/30 January 1915 Venizelos projected a claim to territory in Asia Minor *in excess of 125,000 square kilometres* (Greek text: Th A Vaidis, *Eleftherios Venizelos* [Athens: 1934] pp 186–91).

9. D Chronopoulos, *Dimitrios Gounaris* (Athens: 1987) p 32; Mazower, 'Messiah', p 894.

10. Jonescu, *Some Personal Impressions*, p 244.

11. Pinelopi Delta, *Eleutherios Venizelos: imerologion, anamnisis, martyries, allilografia* ed P A Zannas (Ermis, Athens: 1978) p 13, hereafter Delta, *Venizelos*.

12. Thus reported by Venizelos (in *Vindication*, p 125); variant versions in E S Bagger, *Eminent Europeans* (Putnam, New York: 1922) p 103 and in Prince Nicholas of Greece, *Political memoirs, 1914–1917* (Hutchinson, London: 1928) p 64.

13. Mackenzie, *Greek Memories*, pp 138–56; S Cosmin, *L'Entente et la Grèce pendant la grande guerre* (Paris: 1926) Vol 2, pp 134–52.

14. S B Chester, *Life of Venizelos* (Constable, London: 1921) p 283.

15. Speech at Salonica, 25 November 1916 (Gibbons, *Venizelos*, p 202).

16. Mackenzie, *Greek Memories*, pp 311–16; G Glasgow, *Ronald Burrows: a memoir* (London: 1924) pp 242–51.

17. Hélène Veniselos, *A l'ombre de Veniselos* (Paris: 1955) pp 30–1, hereafter Veniselos, *Ombre*.

18. Granville to Foreign Office, 16 June 1917 (George B Leontaritis, *Greece and the First World War: from neutrality to intervention, 1917–1918* [East European Monographs, Boulder: 1990] p 48).

19. Letter to Georgios Vendiris, 20 April 1931 (Vendiris, *I Ellas*, Vol 2, pp 417–21).

20. Quoted by Leontaritis, *Greece*, p 56. When this remark was made the former Nicholas II had been forced to abdicate and was under house arrest at Tsarskoe Selo.

21. Compare the full translation in *Vindication*, pp 66–161 (pp 148 and 161 for these quotations).

22. Dimitri Kitsikis, *Propagande et pressions en politique internationale: la Grèce et ses revendications à la Conférence de la paix (1919–1920)* (Presses Universitaires de France, Paris: 1963) pp 398–404, hereafter Kitsikis, *Propagande*.

23. Adjusted from the translation in Alexis Dimaras, 'Modernisation and Reaction in Greek Education during the Venizelos Era' in Kitromilides (ed), *Venizelos*, p 319.

24. Alastos, *Venizelos*, p 261.

25. Delta, *Venizelos*, pp 12, 14.

5: Preparing for Paris

1. Romanos to Venizelos, 24 September/7 October 1918; Romanos to Politis, same date (compare the longer translations in Leontaritis, *Greece,* pp 399–400).

2. Interview with M. Venizelos, 15 October 1918 (Lloyd George Papers). Leontaritis, *Greece*, pp 400–12; Petsalis-Diomidis, *Greece*, pp 71–2.

3. Michalakopoulos to Kaklamanos, undated, September 1918 (French text in Kitsikis, *Propagande*, p 399).

4. Venizelos to Lloyd George, 2 November 1918, F/55/1/11 (Lloyd George Papers); text in French in A F Frangoulis, *La Grèce: son statut international, son histoire diplomatique* (Paris: 1934) Vol 2, pp 21–7.

5. S D Spector, *Rumania at the Peace Conference* (New York: 1962) pp 59, 73.

6. N Petsalis-Diomidis, 'Hellenism in Southern Russia and the Ukrainian Campaign: their Effect on the Pontus Question', *Balkan Studies,* 13, ii (1972) pp 221–3.

7. Gibbons, *Venizelos*, pp 179–80; Dafnis, *Sofoklis Venizelos*, p 52.

8. Nicolson, *Peacemaking*, p 341.

9. Veniselos, *Ombre*, pp 80–2.

10. Milner to Fiddes, 16 January 1919 (quoted in Petsalis-Diomidis, *Greece*, p 133).

11. *Local très fréquenté le soir et la nuit, mais où on n'ira pas avec les dames.* Karl Baedeker, *Paris et ses environs*, 17th ed. (Leipzig: 1909) p 16.

12. Nicolson to Vita Sackville-West, 6 July 1919 (J Lees-Milne, *Harold Nicolson* [London: 1980] p 113); Apostolos Alexandris, *Politike anamnisis* (Patras: 1947) pp 128–9.

13. Nicolson, *Peacemaking*, p 223.

14. C Seymour, *Letters from the Paris Peace Conference* (New Haven: 1965) p 56 and note 28. The marginal note was added in 1963.

15. James Barros, 'The Role of Sir Eric Drummond' in *The League of Nations in Retrospect: Proceedings of the Symposium* (De Gruyter, New York: 1983) pp 31–41.

16. Clive Day's diary, 6 January 1919 (quoted in Arthur Walworth, *Wilson and his Peacemakers: American diplomacy at the Paris Peace Conference, 1919* (Norton, New York: 1986) p 61 n. 113).

17. Nicolson, *Peacemaking*, pp 225–6, 228.

18. Nicolson (*Peacemaking*, p 238) quotes Venizelos in French; the English translations in the text are mine.

19. D Lloyd George, *The Truth about the Peace Treaties* (London: 1938) Vol 1, p 214.

6: At the Conference

1. Nicolson, *Peacemaking*, p 240.

2. Nicolson, *Peacemaking*, p 247.

3. Lord Hardinge to Balfour, 21 January 1919 (quoted in Petsalis-Diomidis, *Greece*, p 134).

4. FO 608/37–775 (full text in Petsalis-Diomidis, *Greece*, pp 126–8).

5. Nicolson, *Peacemaking*, p 253; Petsalis-Diomidis, *Greece*, pp 129–30.

6. Nicolson, *Peacemaking*, pp 255–6.

7. Venizelos to Repoulis, 4 February 1919 (compare the longer translation in Petsalis-Diomidis, *Greece*, pp 137–8).

8. Petsalis-Diomidis, *Greece,* pp 138–41; Nicolson, *Peacemaking*, pp 264–5; Frances Stevenson, *Lloyd George: a diary* (Hutchinson, London: 1971) p 172.

9. Nicolson, *Peacemaking*, pp 131, 268, 271–2.

10. Ian Malcolm, *Lord Balfour: a memory* (London: 1930) p 73.

11. Nicolson, *Peacemaking,* pp 275–9; Petsalis-Diomidis, *Greece*, p 176.

12. Petsalis-Diomidis, *Greece*, pp 157–9.

13. Nicolson, *Peacemaking*, p 284; Petsalis-Diomidis, *Greece*, p 177.

14. Nicolson, *Peacemaking*, p 311; Stevenson, *Lloyd George: a diary*, p 173; P C Helmreich, *From Paris to Sèvres* (Ohio State University Press, Columbus: 1974) pp 87–93; Petsalis-Diomidis, *Greece,* pp 157–9; F S Marston, *The Peace Conference of 1919: organisation and procedure* (Oxford: 1944) p 121.

15. Venizelos to Diomidis, 25 January 1919 (summary in English in Petsalis-Diomidis, *Greece*, pp 101–2).

16. Kitsikis, *Propagande,* pp 196–200; www.gec.gr/astir/sept99.htm (retrieved 17 May 2008).

17. Theodoros P Petrakopoulos, *I zoi mou* (Athens: 1961) p 82 (longer quotation in French in Kitsikis, *Propagande*, pp 40–2).

18. *The Times* (London, 24 and 27 March, 2, 9 and 21 April, 26 May 1919); Kitsikis, *Propagande,* pp 253–8.

19. Romanos to Diomidis, 19 May 1919 (Petsalis-Diomidis, *Greece*, pp 159–71).

20. J Fisher, *Curzon and British Imperialism in the Middle East, 1916–19* (London: 1999) p 243.

21. Nicolson, *Peacemaking*, p 323.

22. Nicolson, *Peacemaking*, p 321.

23. Paul Mantoux, *The Deliberations of the Council of Four (March 24-June 28, 1919): notes of the official interpreter*, translated by Arthur S Link. 2

vols (Princeton University Press, Princeton: 1992)
Vol 1, p 483, hereafter Mantoux, *Deliberations*. In
the Dodecanese incident two deaths were confirmed
(Petsalis-Diomidis, *Greece*, pp 201–2 and note 15); Lloyd
George's mention of 'massacres' seems to refer only to
this.

24. Mantoux, *Deliberations*, Vol 1, p 496.

25. 'You have Smyrna': Petsalis-Diomidis, *Greece*, p 203 and
note 19; Petrakopoulos, *I zoi mou*, p 91.

26. Reminiscence by Politis (Kitsikis, *Propagande*,
pp 363–4).

27. Venizelos, *Diary*, 6 May (text in S I Stefanou [ed],
Kimena, Vol 2, pp 575–80).

28. C E Callwell (ed), *Field-Marshal Sir Henry Wilson:
his life and diaries* (London: 1927) Vol 2, pp 189–90,
hereafter Callwell (ed), *Wilson*.

29. Callwell (ed), *Wilson*, Vol 2, p 190; Mantoux,
Deliberations, Vol 1, pp 505–7.

30. Nicolson, *Peacemaking*, p 327.

31. Kaklamanos to Politis, 7 May; Venizelos to Kaklamanos,
8 May (Kitsikis, *Propagande*, pp 360 and 365).

32. Maurice Hankey, *The Supreme Control* (London: 1963)
pp 162–3.

33. Venizelos, *Diary* 7 May.

34. Venizelos, *Diary* 9 May.

35. Venizelos, *Diary* 11 May; Mantoux, *Deliberations*, Vol 2,
pp 36 ff.; Callwell (ed), *Wilson*, Vol 2, p 192.

36. Venizelos, *Diary* 12 May.

37. Callwell (ed) *Wilson*, Vol 2, 192.

38. Callwell (ed), *Wilson*, Vol 2, p 192.

39. Georges Clemenceau, *Grandeurs et misères d'une
victoire* (Plon, Paris: 1930) p 125.

40. Kesaris to Kaklamanos, 15 May 1919 (Kitsikis, *Propagande*, pp 361–3).

41. Venizelos to Kaklamanos, 14 May 1919; Zaharoff to Kaklamanos, 15 May (Kitsikis, *Propagande*, pp 363, 389). Domini Crosfield's family 'homeland' was the Smyrna region. Sir Arthur's reply, carefully mentioning Helena Schilizzi, betrays awareness of her growing interest in Venizelos.

42. Nicolson, *Peacemaking*, p 341.

43. *Organisez rapidement Académie*. The law creating the Athenian Academy was eventually passed on 18 March 1926 during the Pangalos dictatorship (see www.academyofathens.gr/ecportal.asp?id=24&nt=18&lang=2, retrieved 14 May 2008).

44. The meetings are incompletely minuted in Mantoux, *Deliberations*, Vol 2, pp 49–60, partly summarised in Nicolson, *Peacemaking*, pp 332–40 (quotations from both).

45. Mantoux, *Deliberations*, Vol 2, pp 94–100.

46. Nicolson, *Peacemaking*, p 346.

47. Venizelos to Kaklamanos, 30 June 1919 (Kitsikis, *Propagande*, pp 271–2).

48. Mantoux, *Deliberations*, Vol 2, pp 586–9.

49. Petsalis-Diomidis, *Greece*, pp 251–6.

50. Venizelos to Wilson, 22 July 1919; Venizelos to Repoulis, 29 September 1919 (Kitsikis, *Propagande*, p 49; Petsalis-Diomidis, *Greece*, pp 264, 278).

51. C Seymour, *Letters from the Paris Peace Conference*, p 275.

52. Petsalis-Diomidis, *Greece*, pp 265–6.

53. Ian Malcolm, *Lord Balfour: a memory* (London, 1930) p 74.

54. Dafnis, *Sofoklis Venizelos*, pp 56–62.

7: The Catastrophe and the Treaty of Lausanne

1. Alastos, *Venizelos*, p 260; Smith, *Ionian Vision*, p 109.
2. Callwell (ed), *Wilson*, Vol 2, p 213.
3. Kitsikis, *Propagande*, pp 200–1.
4. Callwell (ed), *Wilson*, Vol 2, p 230; Smith, *Ionian Vision*, p 115 (quoting L Paraskevopoulos, *Anamnisis* [Athens: 1933] p 362) and pp 121–2.
5. Burrows to Venizelos, 5 May 1920, as quoted in Richard Clogg, 'Politics and the Academy: Arnold Toynbee and the Koraes Chair', *Middle East Studies* 21, iv (October 1985) p 1.
6. Callwell (ed), *Wilson*, Vol 2, p 245. This was one of the 'Hythe conferences', hosted at Port Lympne by the wealthy MP Philip Sassoon.
7. Smith, *Ionian Vision*, pp 125–6.
8. Callwell (ed), *Wilson*, Vol 2, pp 248–50.
9. Quoted by S Stefanou in his preface to the 1960 edition of Venizelos's Thucydides, p xiv (compare the translation in Evie Holmberg, *Lessons Unlearned: Thucydides and Venizelos on propaganda and the struggle for power* [University of Minnesota, Minneapolis: 2003] p 118).
10. Kitsikis, *Propagande*, p 20.
11. Delta, *Venizelos*, pp 57–60.
12. Callwell (ed), *Wilson*, Vol 2, p 269.
13. Delta, *Venizelos*, p 61.
14. Delta, *Venizelos*, p 10.
15. Alastos, *Venizelos*, p 206.
16. Smith, *Ionian Vision*, pp 184–9.

17. E M House & C Seymour (eds), *What Really Happened at Paris; the story of the Peace Conference, 1918–1919, by American delegates* (Hodder & Stoughton, London: 1921) p 467.

18. Veniselos, *Ombre*, p 37.

19. 'Some Recent Work by Mr. P. A. de László' in *The Studio*, 86 (14 September 1923) pp 128–34.

20. The precise frontier was laid down by the Florence protocol of 27 January 1925 (B Papadakis, *Histoire diplomatique de la question Nord-Epirote* [Athens: 1958] pp 64–92).

21. This is the so-called 'Chanak crisis' (the troops were at Çanakkale). J Lees-Milne, *Harold Nicolson* (London: 1980) p 178.

22. *New York Times*, 29 December 1922; Smith, *Ionian Vision*, pp 329–30.

23. Joseph C Grew, 'The Peace Conference of Lausanne, 1922–1923', *Proceedings of the American Philosophical Society*, 98 (1954) pp 1–10 at p 5, hereafter Grew, 'Lausanne'. For Venizelos's opening address to the Conference see D Kaklamanos, *Eleftherios Venizelos o iros* (Oxford: 1936) pp 29–30 (translation in Alastos, *Venizelos*, p 224).

24. M Llewellyn Smith, 'Venizelos' Diplomacy, 1910–23' in Kitromilides (ed), *Venizelos*, pp 134–92 at p 172.

25. Grew, 'Lausanne', p 10.

26. *Gentlemen! It's peace!* D Kaklamanos, *Eleftherios Venizelos o iros* (Oxford: 1936) p 41; Alastos, *Venizelos*, p 230.

27. Alastos, *Venizelos*, p 229.

28. Mavrogordatos, *Stillborn Republic*, p 199; compare Alastos, *Venizelos*, p 196.

8: Venizelos's Later Career

1. Michalakopoulos to Danglis, 6 September 1922 (adjusted from the translation in Mavrogordatos, *Stillborn Republic*, p 86).

2. On Thucydides 3.62. Compare the longer translation in Holmberg, *Lessons Unlearned*, p 88.

3. On Thucydides 3.37–38 (compare the translation in Holmberg, *Lessons Unlearned*, pp 99–103).

4. Mourellos, *Venizelos*, pp 223–4; http://www.chania. gr/sightshow.jsp?lang=en&id=92 (retrieved 22 March 2008).

5. Veniselos, *Ombre*, pp 58–60. The underlined words are in English in Venizelos's original letter.

6. Quoted by S Stefanou in his preface to the 1960 edition of Venizelos's Thucydides, p xiv (compare the translation in Holmberg, *Lessons Unlearned*, p 118).

7. *Kathimerini* (21 July 1928); for this and other press attacks during the campaign see Mavrogordatos, *Stillborn Republic*, pp 202–5.

8. S Stefanou, *O Venizelos opos ton ezisa apo konta* (Athens: 1974) p 53 (compare the longer translation in Holmberg, *Lessons Unlearned*, p 49).

9. Delta, *Venizelos*, pp 341–8; Paschalis M Kitromilides, 'Venizelos' Intellectual Projects and Cultural Interests' in Kitromilides (ed), *Venizelos*, p 383.

10. Jonescu, *Some Personal Impressions*, p 246.

11. *Kathimerini* (3 March 1931). Compare the longer translation in Mavrogordatos, *Stillborn Republic*, p 59.

12. Veniselos, *Ombre*, pp 60–7.

13. Quoted by S Stefanou in his preface to the 1960 edition of Venizelos's *Thucydides* (compare the translation in Holmberg, *Lessons Unlearned*, p 119).

14. Jonescu, *Some Personal Impressions*, p 247.

15. Mark Mazower, *Greece and the Inter-War Economic Crisis* (Clarendon Press, Oxford: 1991) p 8. Compare Dafnis, *Sofoklis Venizelos*, p 599 n. 25.

16. Delta, *Venizelos*, p 254.

17. Delta, *Venizelos*, p 247; Smith, *Ionian Vision*, pp 156–7.

18. Vendiris, *I Ellas*, Vol 2, p 419.

19. Quoted by S Stefanou in his preface to the 1960 edition of Venizelos's *Thucydides*, p xv (compare the translation in Holmberg, *Lessons Unlearned*, p 119).

20. To Loukas Kanakaris-Roufos, 9 March 1936 (text in Manolikakis, *Venizelos*, p 17).

21. Veniselos, *Ombre*, p 77.

22. Compare the longer translation in Alastos, *Venizelos*, pp 273–4.

23. Apostolos Alexandris, *Politike anamnisis* (Patras: 1947) p 125; compare the longer quotation in French in Kitsikis, *Propagande*, p 51.

24. Quoted by Mark Mazower, *Greece and the Inter-War Economic Crisis* (Oxford, 1991) p 26.

Chronology

YEAR	AGE	THE LIFE AND THE LAND
1864		24 Aug: Eleftherios Venizelos (EV) born at Mournies near Chania (Crete).
1866	2	Anti-Ottoman uprising in Crete (to 1869).
		Venizelos family flees to Cythera and then Syros, returning to Chania in 1872.
1877	13	EV attends commercial school in Athens and gymnasion in Syros (to 1880).
1878	14	Chalepa Pact makes Crete a parliamentary state.
1880	16	EV attends University of Athens Law School.
1886	22	Joseph Chamberlain visits Constantinople and Athens.
		17 Nov: EV publishes interview with Joseph Chamberlain.
1887	23	Jan: EV completes studies; begins law practice.
1888	24	EV edits *Lefka Ori*.
		Liberal majority in Cretan Assembly.
1889	25	15 Apr: EV elected to Cretan Assembly.
		6 May: Assembly votes for union. Ethnic violence; suspension of Assembly.
		Sep: EV flees to Athens.
1891	27	EV marries Maria Katelouzou.

YEAR	HISTORY	CULTURE
1864	Schleswig War. Archduke Maximilian of Austria crowned Emperor of Mexico.	Charles Dickens, *Our Mutual Friend*. Tolstoy, *War and Peace* (-1869).
1866	Austro-Prussian War: Prussian victory at Sadowa: end of German Confederation.	Dostoevsky, *Crime and Punishment*.
1877	Outbreak of Russo-Turkish War.	Henry James, *The American*.
1878	Russo-Turkish War ends.	Thomas Hardy, *The Return of the Native*.
1880	Transvaal Republic declares independence from Britain.	Dostoevsky, *The Brothers Karamazov*.
1886	Irish Home Rule Bill introduced by Prime Minister Gladstone. First Indian National Congress meets.	R L Stevenson, *Dr Jekyll and Mr Hyde*. Frances Hodgson Burnett, *Little Lord Fauntleroy*.
1887	Queen Victoria's Golden Jubilee.	Verdi, opera 'Otello'.
1888	Kaiser Wilhelm II accedes to the throne. Suez Canal convention.	Rudyard Kipling, *Plain Tales from the Hills*.
1889	Austro-Hungarian Crown Prince Rudolf commits suicide at Mayerling. London Dock Strike.	Jerome K Jerome, *Three Men in a Boat*. Richard Strauss, symphonic poem 'Don Juan'.
1891	Young Turk Movement founded in Vienna.	Thomas Hardy, *Tess of the D'Urbervilles*.

YEAR	AGE	THE LIFE AND THE LAND
1893	29	23 Feb: Kyriakos Venizelos born.
1894	30	17 Nov: Sofoklis Venizelos born.
		26 Nov: Maria dies.
1895	31	EV edits *Avgi*.
		Outbreak of new rebellion in Crete.
1897	33	Graeco-Turkish War, in which Greece is rapidly defeated.
		23 Jan: EV joins rebellion at Akrotiri.
		Negotiates with representatives of the Powers.
		10 Nov: EV speaks at Melidoni, urging autonomy as prelude to union.
1898	34	Crete temporarily ruled by Admirals of the four Powers.
		EV on Cretan Executive Committee.
		21 Dec: Prince George, son of King George I of Greece, arrives in Crete as High Commissioner.
1899	35	EV drafts new constitution.
		29 Apr: EV appointed Councillor for Justice in Prince George's cabinet.
1900	36	Oct: Prince George begins first international tour.
1901	37	Feb: Prince George fails to get agreement to union of Crete with Greece.
		31 Mar: EV dismissed. Runs press campaign in *Kiryx* against the Prince's policy.
		1 Jun: EV leads minority in Cretan Assembly.
1902	38	Prince George's second international tour.

YEAR	HISTORY	CULTURE
1893	Franco-Russian alliance signed.	Oscar Wilde, *A Woman of No Importance*.
1894	Sino-Japanese War. Dreyfus Case begins in France.	G & W Grossmith, *The Diary of a Nobody*. Anthony Hope, *The Prisoner of Zenda*.
1895	Armenians massacred in Ottoman Empire.	Tchaikovsky, ballet 'Swan Lake'.
1897	Queen Victoria's Diamond Jubilee. Russia occupies Port Arthur. Zionist Congress in Basel, Switzerland.	H G Wells, *The Invisible Man*. Edmond Rostand, *Cyrano de Bergerac*.
1898	Kitchener defeats Mahdists at Omdurman. Spanish-American War: US gains Cuba, Puerto Rico, Guam and the Philippines. Death of Bismarck.	Thomas Hardy, *Wessex Poems*. Henry James, *The Turn of the Screw*. Oscar Wilde, *The Ballad of Reading Gaol*.
1899	Outbreak of Second Boer War. First Peace Conference at the Hague.	Rudyard Kipling, *Stalky and Co*. Pinero, *Trelawny of the Wells*.
1900	Boxer Rising in China.	Anton Chekhov, *Uncle Vanya*.
1901	Death of Queen Victoria; Edward VII becomes King. Negotiations for Anglo-German alliance end without agreement. First transatlantic radio signal transmitted.	Thomas Mann, *Buddenbrooks*. Strindberg, *Dances of Death*. Rudyard Kipling, *Kim*.
1902	Treaty of Vereeniging ends Second Boer War.	Monet, 'Waterloo Bridge'.

YEAR	AGE	THE LIFE AND THE LAND
1903	39	Prince George gradually loses the support of the Powers.
		Mar: EV is anathematised and briefly imprisoned.
		30 Mar: EV does badly in new elections.
1904	40	Prince George's third international tour.
1905	41	23 Mar: EV leads Revolutionary Assembly at Theriso.
		26 Jun: Deligiannis, Greek Prime Minister, assassinated.
1906	42	Jan: International Committee on reforms in Crete.
		Sep: Prince George replaced by Alexandros Zaimis as High Commissioner.
		EV maintains good relations with Powers and does better in elections: reappointed Councillor for Justice by Zaimis.
1908	44	Jul: Young Turks' ultimatum to Sultan Hamid.
		3 Oct: Zaimis leaves Crete.
		5 Oct: Bulgaria declares independence.
		6 Oct: Austria-Hungary annexes Bosnia.
		7 Oct: EV addresses crowd in Chania, calls for union with Greece.
		8 Oct: EV appointed to executive committee, which 'will act in the name of Greece'.
1909	45	Economic and political crisis in Greece deepens.
		28 Aug: Military League demands reforms.

YEAR	HISTORY	CULTURE
1903	King Alexander I of Serbia murdered. Wright Brothers' first flight.	Henry James, *The Ambassadors*. Film: *The Great Train Robbery*.
1904	Outbreak of Russo-Japanese War.	J M Barrie, *Peter Pan*.
1905	Port Arthur surrenders to Japanese. 'Bloody Sunday' in Russia.	E M Forster, *Where Angels Fear to Tread*. Edith Wharton, *House of Mirth*.
1906	British ultimatum forces Turkey to cede Sinai Peninsula to Egypt. Major earthquake in San Francisco USA kills over 1,000.	John Galsworthy, *A Man of Property*. O Henry, *The Four Million*.
1908	The *Daily Telegraph* publishes remarks about German hostility towards England made by Kaiser Wilhelm II. Union of South Africa is established. Ferdinand I declares Bulgaria's independence and assumes the title of Tsar.	Colette, *La Retraite Sentimentale*. E M Forster, *A Room with a View*. Kenneth Grahame, *The Wind in the Willows*. Anatole France, *Penguin Island*.
1909	Kamil Pasha, grand vizier of Turkey, forced to resign by Turkish nationalists. Plastic (Bakelite) is invented.	H G Wells, *Tono-Bungay*. Marinetti publishes First Futurist Manifesto. Strauss, 'Elektra'.

YEAR	AGE	THE LIFE AND THE LAND
1910	46	Jan–Feb: EV invited by Military League to advise on Greece's problems.
		31 Jan: Stefanos Dragoumis appointed Greek Prime Minister on EV's advice.
		3 Mar: Greek parliament votes for a Revisionist Assembly.
		20 Mar: EV gains majority in Cretan elections.
		21 Aug: EV elected in absentia to Greek Revisionist Assembly.
		16 Sep: Revisionist Assembly meets.
		18 Sep: EV arrives in Athens.
		12 Oct: Stefanos Dragoumis resigns.
		19 Oct: EV appointed Prime Minister of Greece.
1911	47	15 Jun: EV proclaims revised Constitution.
1912	48	Mar: EV leads Liberals to victory in Greek elections.
		May: Italy seizes Dodecanese.
		16 May: EV seals alliance with Bulgaria in preparation for Balkan War.
		Oct: Outbreak of First Balkan War: Greece, Bulgaria, Serbia and Montenegro oppose Ottoman Empire.
		8 Nov: Greek troops enter Salonica.
		16–26 Dec: Inconclusive London Peace Conference.

YEAR	HISTORY	CULTURE
1910	King Edward VII dies; succeeded by George V. Liberals win British General Election. Egyptian Premier Butros Ghali assassinated. South Africa becomes a dominion within the British Empire with Botha as Premier. King Manuel II flees Portugal to England. Portugal is proclaimed a republic. Marie Curie publishes Treatise on Radiography.	E M Forster, *Howard's End*. H G Wells, *The History of Mr. Polly*. Karl May, *Winnetou*. Fernand Leger, 'Nues dans le foret'. Modigliani, 'The Cellist'. Elgar, 'Concerto for Violin in B Minor, Op. 61'. Puccini, 'La Fanciulla del West'. R Vaughan Williams, 'Sea Symphony'.
1911	Agadir crisis.	Saki, *The Chronicles of Clovis*.
1912	*Titanic* sinks; 1,513 die. Woodrow Wilson is elected US President. Lenin establishes connection with Stalin and takes over editorship of *Pravda*.	Alfred Adler, *The Nervous Character*. C G Jung, *The Theory of Psychoanalysis*. Marc Chagall, 'The Cattle Dealer'. Franz Marc, 'Tower of Blue Horses'. Marcel Duchamp, 'Nude descending a staircase II'.

YEAR	AGE	THE LIFE AND THE LAND
1913	49	6 Mar: Greek troops enter Ioannina.
		18 Mar: King George assassinated; succeeded by Constantine I.
		1 Jun: EV signs alliance with Serbia.
		26 Jun: Outbreak of Second Balkan War: Bulgaria opposes Greece and Serbia.
		30 Jul–10 Aug: Bucharest Peace Conference. Greece now assured of Epirus, Macedonia, eastern Aegean islands and Crete.
		6 Dec: Venizelos and King Constantine raise the Greek flag at Chania.
1914	50	6 Aug: EV allows coaling of German warships *Goeben* and *Breslau*.
1915	51	6 Mar: EV resigns over Constantine's rejection of his pro-Entente policy.
		26 Apr: Treaty of London, allying Italy secretly with the Entente.
		12 Jun: EV victorious in elections.
		23 Aug: EV recalled to power.
		23 Sep: Bulgaria mobilises.
		30 Sep: Entente occupation of Salonica begins.
		7 Oct: EV dismissed for opposition to Constantine's policy of neutrality.
		December: Entente occupation of Corfu.
		19 Dec: EV boycotts new elections.

YEAR	HISTORY	CULTURE
1913	US Federal Reserve System is established. Mahatma Gandhi, leader of the Indian Passive Resistance Movement, is arrested.	D H Lawrence, *Sons and Lovers*. Thomas Mann, *Death in Venice*. Grand Central Station in New York is completed.
1914	Archduke Franz Ferdinand of Austria-Hungary and his wife are assassinated in Sarajevo. Outbreak of First World War: Battles of Mons, the Marne and First Ypres; Russians defeated at Battles of Tannenberg and Masurian Lakes.	James Joyce, *Dubliners*. Theodore Dreiser, *The Titan*. Gustav Holst, 'The Planets'. Matisse, 'The Red Studio'. Braque, 'Music'. Film: Charlie Chaplin in *Making a Living*.
1915	First World War: Battles of Neuve Chapelle and Loos. The 'Shells Scandal'. Gallipoli campaign. Germans sink the British liner *Lusitania*, killing 1,198. Germans execute British nurse Edith Cavell in Brussels for harbouring British prisoners.	Joseph Conrad, *Victory*. John Buchan, *The Thirty-Nine Steps*. Ezra Pound, *Cathay*. Duchamp, 'The Large Glass'. Pablo Picasso, 'Harlequin'. Marc Chagall, 'The Birthday'. Max Reger, 'Mozart Variations'. Film: *The Birth of a Nation*.

YEAR	AGE	THE LIFE AND THE LAND
1916	52	26 May: Germans and Bulgarians occupy Fort Rupel.
		Jun: Entente blockade on Greek shipping.
		26 Sep–9 Oct: EV proclaims Provisional Government, first at Chania, finally at Salonica, and declares war on Germany and Bulgaria.
		25 Dec: EV anathematised as traitor.
1917	53	26 Apr: Agreement of Saint-Jean-de-Maurienne on Italy's post-war territorial gains.
		12 Jun: King Constantine abdicates at Entente insistence; succeeded by Alexander.
		27 Jun: EV returns to Athens as Prime Minister under Entente protection.
		24 Aug: EV recalls June 1915 Parliament
		29 Nov–2 Dec: EV, as Entente ally, attends War Council in Paris.
1918	54	30 May: Bulgaria defeated at Skra, largely by Greek forces.
		30 Sep: Bulgaria capitulates.
		Oct–Nov: EV in London and Paris.
		7 Dec: EV sets out for the Peace Conference.
		24 Dec: EV proposed as Chancellor of future League of Nations.
		30 Dec: Produces *Greece before the Peace Congress.*

YEAR	HISTORY	CULTURE
1916	First World War. Battle of Verdun. Battle of the Somme. The Battle of Jutland. US President Woodrow Wilson is re-elected. Wilson issues Peace Note to belligerents in European war. Lloyd George becomes Prime Minister.	Lionel Curtis, *The Commonwealth of Nations*. James Joyce, *Portrait of the Artist as a Young Man*. Vicente Blasco Ibanez, *The Four Horsemen of the Apocalypse*. Film: *Intolerance*.
1917	First World War. February Revolution in Russia. Battle of Passchendaele (Third Ypres). British and Commonwealth forces take Jerusalem. USA declares war on Germany. China declares war on Germany and Russia. German and Russian delegates sign armistice at Brest-Litovsk.	P G Wodehouse, *The Man With Two Left Feet*. T S Eliot, *Prufrock and Other Observations*. Leon Feuchtwanger, *Jud Süss*. Piet Mondrian launches *De Stijl* magazine in Holland. Film: *Easy Street*.
1918	First World War. German Spring offensives on Western Front fail. Allied offensives on Western Front have German army in full retreat. Armistice signed between Allies and Germany; German fleet surrenders. Kaiser Wilhelm II of German abdicates.	Alexander Blok, *The Twelve*. Gerald Manley Hopkins, *Poems*. Luigi Pirandello, *Six Characters in Search of an Author*. Bela Bartok, 'Bluebeard's Castle'. Puccini, 'Il Trittico'.

YEAR	AGE	THE LIFE AND THE LAND
1919	55	3–4 Feb: EV presents Greece's case to the Council of Ten.
		24–6 Feb: EV gives evidence to Greek Committee.
		6–7 May: EV gets approval for Greek occupation of Smyrna.
		15 May: Greek landing at Smyrna.
		29 July: Venizelos-Tittoni pact.
		4 November: King Alexander secretly marries Aspasia Manou.
		27 Nov: EV signs Treaty of Neuilly with Bulgaria.
1920	56	19–26 Apr: San Remo Conference.
		Jul: Greece occupies eastern Thrace.
		13 Aug: Ion Dragoumis killed.
		25 Oct: King Alexander dies; replaced by Admiral Koundouriotis as Regent.
		14 Nov: EV loses election decisively.
		17 Nov: EV leaves Athens, eventually settling in Paris.
1921	57	10 Jul: New Greek offensive in Anatolia.
		15 Sep: EV marries Helena Schilizzi.
		9 Nov: Greece loses northern Epirus when Albania's 1913 frontiers are confirmed.

YEAR	HISTORY	CULTURE
1919	Communist Revolt in Berlin. Paris Peace Conference adopts principle of founding League of Nations. Benito Mussolini founds Fascist movement in Italy. Peace Treaty of Versailles signed. US Senate votes against ratification of Versailles Treaty, leaving the USA outside the League of Nations.	Bauhaus movement founded by Walter Gropius. Kandinsky, 'Dreamy Improvisation'. Paul Klee, 'Dream Birds'. Thomas Hardy, *Collected Poems*. Herman Hesse, *Demian*. George Bernard Shaw, *Heartbreak House*. Film: *The Cabinet of Dr Caligari*.
1920	League of Nations comes into existence. League of Nations headquarters moved to Geneva. Warren G Harding wins US Presidential election. Bolsheviks win Russian Civil War. Adolf Hitler announces his 25-point programme in Munich.	F Scott Fitzgerald, *This Side of Paradise*. Franz Kafka, *The Country Doctor*. Katherine Mansfield, *Bliss*. Rambert School of Ballet formed. Lyonel Feininger, 'Church'.
1921	Paris Conference of wartime allies fixes Germany's reparation payments. Irish Free State established. Washington Naval Treaty signed.	Max Ernst, 'The Elephant Celebes'. Aldous Huxley, *Chrome Yellow*. D H Lawrence, *Women in Love*. Prokofiev, 'The Love for Three Oranges'.

YEAR	AGE	THE LIFE AND THE LAND
1922	58	26 Aug: Greek front gives way at Afyonkarahisar.
		9 Sep: Turkish army retakes Smyrna.
		27 Sep: King Constantine abdicates and is replaced by King George II.
		28 Nov: Executions at Goudi.
1923	59	30 Jan: EV signs population exchange convention with İsmet (İnönü).
		24 Jul: EV signs Treaty of Lausanne.
		19 Dec: George II goes into exile in Romania; replaced by Koundouriotis as regent.
1924	60	11 Jan: EV appointed Prime Minister.
		6 Feb: EV resigns Premiership.
		10 Mar: EV leaves for Paris, where he works on Thucydides.
		25 Mar: After referendum Koundouriotis becomes president of Greek Republic.
1925	61	25 Jun: Theodoros Pangalos appointed Prime Minister.
1926	62	15 Mar–24 Aug: Pangalos becomes self-appointed President.
1927	63	EV returns to live in Chania.

YEAR	HISTORY	CULTURE
1922	Gandhi sentenced to six years in prison for civil disobedience. Election in Irish Free State gives majority to Pro-Treaty candidates. IRA takes large areas under its control. League of Nations council approves British mandate in Palestine.	T S Eliot, *The Waste Land*. James Joyce, *Ulysses*. British Broadcasting Company (later Corporation) (BBC) founded: first radio broadcasts. Film: *Dr. Mabuse the Gambler*.
1923	French and Belgian troops occupy the Ruhr when Germany fails to make reparation payments. The USSR formally comes into existence.	François Mauriac, *Genitrix*. P G Wodehouse, *The Inimitable Jeeves*. George Gershwin, 'Rhapsody in Blue'.
1924	Death of Lenin. Dawes Plan published. Turkish National Assembly expels the Ottoman dynasty. Greece is proclaimed a republic. Labour Party loses general election after *Daily Mail* publishes the Zinoviev Letter.	Noel Coward, *The Vortex*. E M Forster, *A Passage to India*. Thomas Mann, *The Magic Mountain*. George Bernard Shaw, *St Joan*.
1925	Locarno Treaty signed in London.	Film: *Battleship Potemkin*.
1926	General Strike in Great Britain.	Ernest Hemingway, *The Sun Also Rises*.
1927	Inter-Allied military control of Germany ends.	Film: *The Jazz Singer*.

YEAR	AGE	THE LIFE AND THE LAND
1928	64	23 May: EV resumes Liberal leadership.
		4 Jul: EV appointed Prime Minister.
		19 Aug: EV gains sweeping election victory.
1929	65	Mar: EV signs co-operation treaty with Yugoslavia.
		9 Dec: Zaimis replaces Koundouriotis as President.
1930	66	Oct: EV signs cooperation treaty with Turkey in Ankara.
1932	68	25 Sep: Knife-edge election result.
		3 Nov: EV resigns Premiership.
1933	69	16 Jan: EV appointed Prime Minister.
		5 Mar: EV loses election heavily.
		6 Jun: EV attacked in assassination attempt; Helena wounded.
1935	71	1 Mar: EV is figurehead of mismanaged coup; flees to Italy and eventually Paris; is sentenced to death in absentia.
		3 Nov: George II returns.
1936	72	13 Apr: Ioannis Metaxas appointed Prime Minister.
		18 Mar: EV dies in Paris.

YEAR	HISTORY	CULTURE
1928	Albania is proclaimed a Kingdom.	D H Lawrence, *Lady Chatterley's Lover*.
	Plebiscite in Germany against building new battleships fails.	Aldous Huxley, *Point Counterpoint*.
	Alexander Fleming discovers Penicillin.	George Gershwin, 'An American in Paris'.
1929	Germany accepts Young Plan at Reparations.	Erich Maria Remarque, *All Quiet on the Western Front*.
	The Wall Street Crash.	Noel Coward, *Bittersweet*.
1930	London Naval Treaty.	W H Auden, *Poems*.
1932	F D Roosevelt wins US Presidential election.	Brecht, *St Joan of the Slaughterhouses*.
		Films: *Grand Hotel. Tarzan the Ape Man*.
1933	Adolf Hitler is appointed Chancellor of Germany.	George Orwell, *Down and Out in Paris and London*.
	Germany withdraws from League of Nations and Disarmament Conference.	Films: *Duck Soup. King Kong. Queen Christina*.
1935	Saarland is incorporated into Germany following a plebiscite.	T S Eliot, *Murder in the Cathedral*.
	League of Nations imposes sanctions against Italy following its invasion of Abyssinia.	Emlyn Williams, *Night Must Fall*.
		Films: *The 39 Steps. Top Hat*.
	German troops occupy Rhineland.	J M Keynes, *General Theory of Employment, Interest and Money*.
	Outbreak of Spanish Civil War.	Films: *Camille. Things to Come*.

Further Reading

First, the Peace Conference itself. Margaret Macmillan, *Paris 1919: six months that changed the world* (Murray, London: 2001) is a fresh view of the main players at Paris. Chapter 25 focuses on Venizelos, Chapter 29 on the occupation of Smyrna. Note Robert Lansing's *The Big Four and Others of the Peace Conference* (Houghton Mifflin, Boston: 1921), with a sketch of Venizelos; the collective volume by the U S experts, E M House & C Seymour (eds), *What Really Happened at Paris; the Story of the Peace Conference, 1918–1919, by American Delegates* (Hodder & Stoughton, London: 1921); and two other more recent works, Paul C Helmreich, *From Paris to Sèvres: the Partition of the Ottoman Empire at the Peace Conference of 1919–1920* (Ohio State University Press, Columbus: 1974) and Arthur Walworth, *Wilson and his Peacemakers: American Diplomacy at the Paris Peace Conference, 1919* (Norton, New York: 1986).

Paul Mantoux, *The Deliberations of the Council of Four (March 24-June 28, 1919): Notes of the Official Interpreter* translated by Arthur S Link. 2 vols (Princeton University Press, Princeton: 1992) is a fairly full record of those crucial meetings.

There are two essential books on the work of the Greek delegation in Paris. Dimitri Kitsikis, *Propagande et pressions en politique internationale: la Grèce et ses revendications à la Conférence de la paix (1919–1920)* (Presses Universitaires de France, Paris: 1963) ['Propaganda and pressures in international politics: Greece and her claims at the Peace Conference, 1919–1920'] is a study in French, full of insights into the activities in Paris in 1919 of Venizelos himself, the official delegation, the various groups of 'unredeemed Greeks' and their propagandists. N Petsalis-Diomidis, *Greece at the Paris Peace Conference (1919)* (Institute for Balkan Studies, Salonica: 1978) is a well-documented and impartial narrative of the Greek negotiations; also covered in some detail are the preceding discussions in Rome (pp 62–3, 76–84, 109–15). Add to these Harold Nicolson, *Peacemaking 1919* (Constable, London: 1933), a personal diary and commentary describing many encounters with Venizelos; and Stephen Bonsal, *Suitors and Suppliants: the Little Nations at Versailles* (Prentice-Hall, New York: 1946). Chapter 11 deals with Metropolitan Chrysanthos and the Pontic Greeks, on whom further light is shed by Kitsikis, *Propagande et pressions* pp 417–22. Nicolson also wrote *Curzon: the last phase* (Constable, London: 1934), covering the Lausanne conference of 1922–3.

As the Paris Conference opened Venizelos circulated his own compilation, *La Grèce devant le Congrès de la Paix* (Paris: 1919), translated as *Greece before the Peace Congress* (Oxford University Press, New York: 1919). This is not to be confused with the pseudonymous propaganda volume *Greece Before the Conference, by Polybius* (Allen & Unwin, London: 1919), written by Dimitrios Kalopothakis.

There is no full biography of Venizelos in English. Nearly 70 years have passed since 'Doros Alastos' published

Venizelos, Patriot, Statesman, Revolutionary (Lund Humphries, London: 1942). The author, a Cypriot journalist whose real name was Evdoros Ioannidis, aimed to evoke sympathy for Greece under German occupation.

First among early biographers was the Greek journalist Kostas Kairofylas with *Eleftherios Venizelos: his life and work* (London: 1915); the most useful section concerns the negotiations in London and Bucharest in 1913, which Kairofylas reported on the spot. Of the four sketches and biographies published between 1917 and 1921 the best is H A Gibbons, *Venizelos* (T Fisher Unwin, London: 1921), with useful sidelights on wartime Greece.

Nearly 20 years after Venizelos's death his second wife published a brief memoir in French: Hélène Veniselos, *A l'ombre de Veniselos* (Paris: 1955) ['In the shadow of Venizelos']. What little she says of Greek politics is unreliable; as to their personal life, the memoir is interesting not least for what it leaves out.

In 2006 Paschalis M Kitromilides edited what is by no means a full biography, but is an extremely useful and up-to-date collection of papers on aspects of Venizelos's life and career: *Eleftherios Venizelos: the trials of statesmanship* (Edinburgh University Press, Edinburgh: 2006), referred to elsewhere as 'Kitromilides, *Venizelos*'.

The biographies in Greek are too numerous to list here in full. Useful, though already outdated in some details, is the well-documented study of Venizelos's early years by Lili Makraki, *Eleftherios Venizelos 1864–1910: i diaplasi enos ethnikou igeti* (Athens: 1992) ['Eleftherios Venizelos 1864–1910: the building of a national leader']. This is based on Makraki's American dissertation and is partly available in two articles in English (note the English forms of her name):

A Lily Macrakis, 'Eleftherios Venizelos: Crete, 1864–1910: the main problems' in A Lily Macrakis and P N Diamandouros (eds), *New trends in Modern Greek Historiography* (Hanover, NH: 1982) pp 85–98; A Lilly Macrakis, 'Venizelos' Early Life and Political Career in Crete, 1864–1910' in Kitromilides, *Venizelos* pp 37–84.

Available books on Venizelos's private life draw partly on documents, partly on family memories and oral history. Makraki has added important details to this still-living tradition, which is otherwise best represented by two rich but undigested volumes in Greek: Giannis Mourellos, *Venizelos: i agapes tou, i chares tou, i odynes tou* (Athens: 1964) ['Venizelos: his loves, his joys, his sorrows']; Giannis Manolikakis, *Eleftherios Venizelos: i agnosti zoi tou* (Gnosi, Athens: 1985) ['Eleftherios Venizelos: his unknown life']. Further Greek biographical sources include the following. Pinelopi Delta, *Eleutherios Venizelos: imerologion, anamnisis, martyries, allilografia*, ed P A Zannas (Ermis, Athens: 1978) ['Eleutherios Venizelos: diary, memoirs, testimonies, correspondence'], edited from Penelope Delta's manuscripts, it arranges contemporary diary entries alongside reminiscences that were written many years later. Kyriakos Mitsotakis, *Ta mikra chronia enos megalou: i mathitiki zoi tou Eleftheriou Venizelou* (Minos, Athens: 1972) ['The childhood of a great man: the schooldays of Eleftherios Venizelos'] publishes surviving correspondence between him, his father and his teachers. Dimitrios Kaklamanos, *Eleftherios Venizelos o iros* (Oxford: 1936) ['Eleftherios Venizelos the hero'] is an admiring memoir of Venizelos at Lausanne. Grigorios Dafnis, *Sofoklis Eleftheriou Venizelos* (Ikaros, Athens: 1970) is an exhaustive biography of Venizelos's second son, later Prime Minister.

Few of Venizelos's political texts are available in English.

His interminable parliamentary speech of August 1917 is in *The Vindication of Greek National Policy, 1912–1917: a report of speeches delivered in the Greek chamber, August 23 to 26, 1917, by Mr E Venizelos and others, with an introduction by J Gennadius* (Allen & Unwin, London: 1918). His writings and speeches from his first intervention in Greece until his final exile have been collected in Greek in four volumes: S I Stefanou (ed), *Ta kimena tou Eleftheriou Venizelou, 1909–1935* (Leschi Fileleftheron, Athens: 1981–1984) ['The texts of Eleftherios Venizelos, 1909–1935']. This includes (Vol 2 pp 575–80) his brief diary of events in Paris during May 1919. His historical articles of 1934 and 1935, rehearsing the old quarrels of the National Schism and warning of future civil war, are found in Greek (alongside Ioannis Metaxas's responses) in: E Venizelos and I Metaxas, *I istoria tou ethnikou dichasmou* (Kyromanos, Salonica: 2003) ['The history of the National Schism']. Venizelos's history of the 1889 Cretan rebellion is in: Ioannis G Manolikakis (ed) *Eleftheriou Venizelou i kritiki epanastasis tou 1889* (Aptera, Athens: 1971) ['The Cretan uprising of 1889']. His translation of Thucydides was published soon after his death: Dimitrios Kaklamanos (ed) *Thoukydidou istoriai kata metaphrasin Eleftheriou Venizelou* (Oxford: 1937–40); his accompanying notes are available in Evi Zachariadi-Holmberg (ed), *Ta scholia tou Venizelou ston Thoukydidi* (Athens: 1991) ['Venizelos's commentary on Thucydides'], and there is a study of them in English (note the English form of the author's name): Evie Holmberg, *Lessons Unlearned: Thucydides and Venizelos on Propaganda and the Struggle for Power* (University of Minnesota, Minneapolis: 2003).

R F Holland, 'Nationalism, Ethnicity and the Concert of Europe: the case of the High Commissionership of Prince and 1922 note also Thanos Veremis, *The military in Greek politics: from independence to democracy* (London: 1997). There is a mass of detail in Georgios Vendiris, *I Ellas tou 1910–1920: istoriki meleti*, 2 vols (Athens: 1931) ['Greece of 1910–1920: historical study']; the author was a Venizelist and close friend. Michael Llewellyn Smith, 'Venizelos' Diplomacy, 1910–23: from Balkan alliance to Greek-Turkish settlement' in Kitromilides, *Venizelos* pp 134–192 is helpful on what went before the Paris negotiations and what followed. George B Leon, *Greece and the Great Powers, 1914–1917* (Institute for Balkan Studies, Salonica: 1974), a political history of the first three wartime years, is followed by a sequel written by the same author under a different name: George B Leontaritis, *Greece and the First World War: from Neutrality to Intervention, 1917–1918* (East European Monographs, Boulder: 1990). Michael Llewellyn Smith, *Ionian Vision: Greece in Asia Minor, 1919–1922* (Allen Lane, London: 1973) is a compelling narrative of the Asia Minor adventure leading up to the 1922 catastrophe and the executions at Goudi; note also pp 12–18 on the discussions with Stavridi and Lloyd George in London in December 1912. Supplementing this is A A Pallis, *Greece's Anatolian Venture and After: a survey of the diplomatic and political aspects of the Greek expedition to Asia Minor (1915–1922)* (Methuen, London: 1937), a readable history of events before and after the 1922 catastrophe; and D Pentzopoulos, *The Balkan Exchange of Minorities and its Impact upon Greece* (Mouton, Paris: 1962). For the 1920s and 1930s see Mark Mazower, *Greece and the Inter-War Economic Crisis* (Clarendon Press, Oxford: 1991) and George Mavrogordatos, *Stillborn Republic: Social Conditions and Party Strategy in Greece 1922–1936* (University of California Press, Berkeley: 1983), a perceptive study focusing on party allegiances and voting patterns. Robert Holland and Diana Markides, *The British and the Hellenes: struggles for mastery in the eastern Mediterranean 1850–1960* (Oxford University Press, Oxford: 2006) is good on Crete and Cyprus.

Picture Sources

The author and publishers wish to express their thanks to the following sources of illustrative material and/or permission to reproduce it. They will make proper acknowledgements in future editions in the event that any omissions have occurred.

Topham Picturepoint: pp viii, xvi, 76 and 142.

Endpapers
The Signing of Peace in the Hall of Mirrors, Versailles, 28th June 1919 by Sir William Orpen (Imperial War Museum: akg Images)
Front row: Dr Johannes Bell (Germany) signing with Herr Hermann Müller leaning over him
Middle row (seated, left to right): General Tasker H Bliss, Col E M House, Mr Henry White, Mr Robert Lansing, President Woodrow Wilson (United States); M Georges Clemenceau (France); Mr David Lloyd George, Mr Andrew Bonar Law, Mr Arthur J Balfour, Viscount Milner, Mr G N Barnes (Great Britain); Prince Saionji (Japan)
Back row (left to right): M Eleftherios Venizelos (Greece);

Dr Afonso Costa (Portugal); Lord Riddell (British Press);
Sir George E Foster (Canada); M Nikola Pašić (Serbia);
M Stephen Pichon (France); Col Sir Maurice Hankey,
Mr Edwin S Montagu (Great Britain); the Maharajah of
Bikaner (India); Signor Vittorio Emanuele Orlando (Italy);
M Paul Hymans (Belgium); General Louis Botha (South
Africa); Mr W M Hughes (Australia)

Jacket images

(Front): Imperial War Museum; akg Images.
(Back): *Peace Conference at the Quai d'Orsay* by Sir William
Orpen (Imperial War Museum: akg Images).
Left to right (seated): Signor Orlando (Italy); Mr Robert
Lansing, President Woodrow Wilson (United States); M
Georges Clemenceau (France); Mr David Lloyd George, Mr
Andrew Bonar Law, Mr Arthur J Balfour (Great Britain);
Left to right (standing): M Paul Hymans (Belgium); Mr
Eleftherios Venizelos (Greece); The Emir Feisal (The
Hashemite Kingdom); Mr W F Massey (New Zealand);
General Jan Smuts (South Africa); Col E M House (United
States); General Louis Botha (South Africa); Prince Saionji
(Japan); Mr W M Hughes (Australia); Sir Robert Borden
(Canada); Mr G N Barnes (Great Britain); M Ignacy
Paderewski (Poland)

Index

NB All family relationships are to Eleftherios Venizelos unless otherwise stated.

A

Alastos, Doros 11

Albania 55, 63, 66, 80, 84, 88, 98, 100, 108, 118, 135, 140

Alexander, King 70, 71, 124, 127, 128–9, 154

Alexandris, Apostolos 29, 42, 44, 45, 69, 73, 93–4, 140, 149, 156

Andrew, Prince 138

Armenia 55, 85, 91–2, 116, 139, 155

Atatürk *see* Mustafa Kemal

Austria-Hungary 30, 56–7, 63, 64, 73, 120

B

Balfour, Arthur 92, 108, 114, 116, 119–20

Balkan Wars, the 47–53

Belgium 98

Benakis, Emmanouil 39, 42, 61, 69, 131, 136

Biliotti, Alfred 11, 13, 14

Blum, Athanasios 29

Blum, Paraskevoula 29, 40, 54, 135

Bosnia and Herzegovina 29, 30

Bourchier, J D 37, 47

Bucharest, Treaty of 52, 55, 68, 89, 95

Bulgaria 23, 29, 30, 47–52, 57–9, 60–5, 67, 79, 80, 86, 89, 95, 100, 105, 112, 119, 120, 126, 138, 139, 147, 157, 159

Burrows, Ronald 68, 106–7, 118, 126

C

Cambon, Jules 103
Cecil, Lord Robert 95, 101
Chamberlain, Joseph 9–11, 41
Chatzanestis, General 137
Chrysanthos of Trebizond, Metropolitan 91
Churchill, Winston 49, 125
Clemenceau, Georges 75, 84, 87, 93–4, 98, 107–8, 110–17, 120, 125
Constantine, King 31, 33, 34, 35, 45–8, 51–3, 56–8, 60, 61, 63, 66, 69–71, 129, 132, 137
Council of Four, the 107–8, 112, 117
Council of Ten, the 96, 101, 105, 107, 109
Crete 3–5, 6–17, 18–32, 34, 37, 39, 40, 42, 46, 50, 54, 67, 87, 153–4, 157, 158–9
Crosfield, Dominiki 49
Curzon, Lord 108, 112, 137–9
Cyprus 49, 63, 81, 89, 92, 97, 98, 101–3, 116, 151, 158

D

Danglis, Panagiotis 33, 53, 66–7, 73, 102, 145–6
Day, Clive 94, 96, 100–3, 104, 105
Deligiannis, Theodoros 27
Delta, Penelope 61, 129, 154, 159
Dillon, Emile Joseph 91
Diomidis, Alexandros 42, 68, 87, 96, 148
Dousmanis, Viktor 70
Dragoumis, Ion 60, 70, 128
Dragoumis, Stefanos 29, 36–7, 42, 70
Dutasta, Paul 93

D

Egypt 24, 85
Elliot, Sir Francis 36
Evmenios, Metropolitan 24

F

Ferdinand of Romania, King 52
First World War, the 56–75, 79–87
Foumis, Kostis 6, 12, 13, 14, 21, 23, 25, 147
Four Principles, the 84, 100
Fournet, Admiral Dartige du 69

Fourteen Points, the 80,
    82–3, 100
France 10, 56, 58, 62, 65, 70,
    74, 85, 87, 88, 96, 102–3,
    107, 113, 119, 134, 138,
    156

G

Gavriilidis, Vlasis 61
Gennadios, Ioannis 73, 86
Gennadis, Nikolaos 15
George I, King 16, 23, 47,
    51
George II, King 70, 137,
    145, 155, 157
George, Prince 19, 21–3, 25,
    29, 34, 37, 154
Gladstone, William 11
Glinos, Dimitris 68, 74
Gonatas, Stylianos 146
Gounaris, Dimitrios 29, 61,
    70, 133–4, 137, 146
Granville, Lord 68, 70
Great Britain 10, 19, 49, 56,
    58, 62, 65, 69, 70, 74, 81,
    85, 88–9, 92, 96, 98, 102,
    107, 108, 116–17, 119,
    125, 134, 136, 138, 149,
    151, 153, 158
Greece
    Balkan Wars, and
        47–53

delegation to Paris
    87–92
demands at Paris 79–89,
    94–7, 98–121
First World War, and
    56–75, 79–87
occupation of Asia
    Minor 104–17, 122–7,
    132–6
Second World War, and
    157
Grew, Joseph 138, 140
Gryparis, Ioannis 12–13,
    42, 47–8

H

House, Colonel Edward
    84–5, 93, 105, 119

I

Iliakis, Giankos 155
India 117
Ionescu, Tache 49–50, 51,
    52, 59, 61, 86, 104, 151,
    158
Iraq 85
Italy 6, 10, 46, 62, 66, 69,
    79, 88–9, 96, 98, 101, 103,
    108–10, 113, 118–19, 133,
    134, 135, 138, 141
    Greco-Italian treaty
        127

İsmet İnönü 138–40
İzmir *see* Smyrna

J
Japan 29, 96, 138
Jonnart, Charles 70–1

K
Kafandaris, Georgios 146, 148, 152
Kaklamanos, Dimitrios 50, 73, 85, 86, 87, 92, 95, 98, 106, 112, 115–18, 124, 138, 140
Kalogeropoulos, Nikolaos 133
Kalopothakis, Dimitrios 106
Karamanlis, Konstantinos 158
Kerofylas, Konstantinos 64, 91
Kerr, Philip 117, 133
Kesaris, Christos 115
Koromilas, Lampros 42, 47–8, 69, 73
Koumoundouros, Alexandros 7–8
Koundouriotis, Pavlos 48, 66–7, 129, 148
Koundouros, Manousos 14, 19, 21, 27, 28, 39

Kyrou, Alexis 151

L
Lausanne, Treaty of 137–41, 145, 158
League of Nations, the 81, 94–5, 101, 135, 155
Lloyd George, David 49, 74, 81–2, 84–6, 92–7, 102, 104, 107–18, 123, 125–6, 129, 132–3, 137
London, Treaty of 62
Lybyer, Albert 100–1
Lympne Conference, the 126

M
Macedonia 30, 34, 48, 50–2, 64, 67, 80–1, 111, 159
Makkas, Leon 85
Manolikakis, Ioannis 11
Manos, Konstantinos 26, 39
Markantonakis, Klearchos 6, 41, 135
Mavromichalis, Kyriakoulis 34–7
Melas, Leon 136
Metaxas, Ioannis 43–6, 49, 50, 53, 60–1, 66, 70, 145, 152, 153–4, 157–8

Mexborough, Lady 121
Michalakopoulos, Andreas 73, 85, 86, 101, 138, 145–6, 149
Military League, the 33–6, 66
Millerand, Alexandre 125
Milner, Lord 92
Mitsotakis, Konstantinos 7, 12
Montenegro 48–9
Murat, Princess 94
Mussolini, Benito 149–50, 154, 157
Mustafa Kemal (Atatürk) 122–3, 133, 134, 137

N

Nicholas, Prince 151
Nicolson, Harold 96, 100, 101, 102–5, 108–9, 112, 116–17, 133, 136
Noel, Irene 49

O

Orlando, Vittorio 88–9, 108–9, 111, 112–14, 118
Ottoman Empire, the 3–4, 9–10, 14–15, 19, 23, 29–31, 33, 37, 46–52, 55–8, 60, 79–80, 85–6, 122, 125, 127, 132, 159

P

Paderewski, Ignacy 135
Palestine 85
Pangalos, Theodoros 31–2, 146
Papadiamantopoulos, Andreas 24, 26, 27
Papanastasiou, Alexandros 145, 146, 152
Papandreou, Andreas 158
Papandreou, Georgios 148–9, 157
Paraskevopoulos, Leonidas 54, 108, 111, 115
Paris Peace Conference, the 84–6, 90–7, 98–121
Greek delegation 87–92
Pašić, Nikola 86
Passaris, Michail 32
Paul, Prince 129, 154
Petrakopoulos, Theodoros 106
Pichon, Stephen 101
Plastiras, Nikolaos 137, 145–6, 152–4
Politis, Nikolaos 68, 85, 87–8, 91–2, 101, 106, 107, 110, 117, 135
Polk, Frank L 119
Polychronopoulos, Ioannis 153

R

Rallis, Dimitrios 27, 31,
  33–4, 37, 40, 130, 132,
  133
Rallis, Georgios 158
Rallis, Ioannis 157
Repoulis, Emmanouil 29,
  42, 55, 87, 96, 102, 103,
  111, 117, 119, 122, 129,
  131
Riza Nour Bey 138
Romania 50, 51–2, 59–60,
  86, 138, 140
Romanos, Athos 73, 81, 90,
  108
Russia 10, 15–16, 19, 29, 34,
  56, 65, 70, 79, 87

S

Said Halim 56
Saint Germain, Treaty of
  120
Saint-Jean-de-Maurienne
  88
Salonica 30, 48, 50, 51,
  52, 62–9, 72, 73, 74, 81,
  108, 111, 115, 132, 146,
  149–50
San Remo Conference, the
  125–6
Sarrail, General Maurice
  62, 65, 66, 67

Schilizzi, Helena *see* Helena
  Venizelos
Schliemann, Heinrich 47
Second World War, the 157
Serbia 48–52, 56–60, 62, 63,
  65, 86, 98, 138
Sévres, Treaty of 127–8,
  132, 135
Seymour, Charles 94
Sfakianakis, Ioannis 17, 19,
  20
Skouloudis, Manolis 147
Skouloudis, Stefanos 63,
  65, 72
Smyrna (İzmir) 12, 59, 79,
  81, 83, 86, 87, 88, 100–1,
  103, 104, 106–17, 122–3,
  125, 127, 128, 132, 136,
  139, 141
Sofoulis, Themistoklis 128,
  146, 155
Sonnino, Sidney 88–9, 98,
  100, 101
Spa Conference, the 127
Spanoudis, Konstantinos
  73, 85
Stavridi, John 49, 68, 93, 94,
  118, 132
Steed, Wickham 91
Stergiadis, Aristidis 122
Stevenson, Frances 105,
  114

Streit, Georgios 53, 56, 57, 70
Supreme Council, the 107,
    110, 120, 122, 127
Syria 85

T

Talbot, Commander Gerald
    88, 95, 100, 107, 137–8
Tevfik Bedri Bey 14
Theoklitos, Metroploitan
    69
Theotokis, Georgios 30–1,
    37, 40, 42, 43, 45
Tittoni, Tommaso 118–19,
    135
Trikoupis, Charilaos 7, 13,
    17
Tsaldaris, Panagis 146,
    152–3
Tsatsos, Konstantinos 96

U

Ukraine, the 87, 98, 111–12,
    159
United States of America,
    the 79–81, 85, 87, 89, 92,
    94–6, 100–1, 103–7, 109,
    113, 119, 135, 138, 156

V

Venizelos, Agathoklis
    (brother) 5, 8, 14

Venizelos, Ekaterina (sister)
    7
Venizelos, Eleftherios
    assassination attempts on
        127–8, 152–3
    Cretan career 11–17,
        18–33
    death 155
    early life 5–8
    Greek politics 33–54,
        55–66
    Joseph Chamberlain,
        meeting with 9–11
    later career 145–55
    Lausanne Conference, at
        the 137–41
    'National Schism', and
        56–66
    occupation of Asia
        Minor, and the
        104–17, 122–7, 132–6
    Paris Peace Conference,
        at the 84–5, 90–7,
        98–120
    Salonica government,
        and 66–75
Venizelos, Eleftherios
    (grandson) 146
Venizelos, Evanthia (sister)
    6, 8, 25
Venizelos, Helena (2nd
    wife) 49, 68, 131, 134–6,

147–8, 150, 151, 152–3, 154–6

Venizelos, Kyriakos (father) 4–8

Venizelos, Kyriakos (son) 13, 19, 25, 28, 39, 43, 87, 135, 146, 153, 156

Venizelos, Maria (1st wife) 12, 13–14

Venizelos, Sofoklis (son) 13, 19, 25, 28, 39, 43, 48, 68, 81, 87–8, 121, 125, 127, 128, 131, 135, 156, 157

Venizelos, Styliani (mother) 5

Versailles, Treaty of 120

Vlachos, Georgios 149, 151, 158

W

Wilhelm II, Kaiser 46, 53, 56–7

Wilson, General Sir Henry 111, 115, 123, 125–7, 129

Wilson, Woodrow 80, 84–5, 89, 93, 94–5, 100, 102–5, 107–8, 110–16, 118–20, 156

Y

Yugoslavia 150

Z

Zaharoff, Sir Basil 94, 110, 116

Zaimis, Alexandros 28, 30, 37, 63, 65, 70, 71, 148

Zervos, Skevos 109

Zervoudakis, Emmanouil 121

UK PUBLICATION: November 2008 to December 2010
CLASSIFICATION: Biography/History/
    International Relations
FORMAT: 198 × 128mm
EXTENT: 208pp
ILLUSTRATIONS: 6 photographs plus 4 maps
TERRITORY: world

Chronology of life in context, full index, bibliography, innovative layout
with sidebars

Woodrow Wilson: United States of America by Brian Morton
Friedrich Ebert: Germany by Harry Harmer
Georges Clemenceau: France by David Watson
David Lloyd George: Great Britain by Alan Sharp
Prince Saionji: Japan by Jonathan Clements
Wellington Koo: China by Jonathan Clements
Eleftherios Venizelos: Greece by Andrew Dalby
From the Sultan to Atatürk: Turkey by Andrew Mango
The Hashemites: The Dream of Arabia by Robert McNamara
Chaim Weizmann: The Dream of Zion by Tom Fraser
Piip, Meierovics & Voldemaras: Estonia, Latvia & Lithuania by Charlotte Alston
Ignacy Paderewski: Poland by Anita Prazmowska
Beneš, Masaryk: Czechoslovakia by Peter Neville
Károlyi & Bethlen: Hungary by Bryan Cartledge
Karl Renner: Austria by Jamie Bulloch
Vittorio Orlando: Italy by Spencer Di Scala
Pašić & Trumbić: The Kingdom of Serbs, Croats and Slovenes by Dejan Djokic
Aleksandŭr Stamboliĭski: Bulgaria by R J Crampton
Ion Bratianu: Romania by Keith Hitchin
Paul Hymans: Belgium by Sally Marks
General Smuts: South Africa by Antony Lentin
William Hughes: Australia by Carl Bridge
William Massey: New Zealand by James Watson
Sir Robert Borden: Canada by Martin Thornton
Maharajah of Bikaner: India by Hugh Purcell
Afonso Costa: Portugal by Filipe Ribeiro de Meneses
Epitácio Pessoa: Brazil by Michael Streeter
South America by Michael Streeter
Central America by Michael Streeter
South East Asia by Andrew Dalby
The League of Nations by Ruth Henig
Consequences of Peace: The Versailles Settlement – Aftermath and Legacy
    by Alan Sharp